S0-AJV-210

Garfield MINUS Garfield

BY JIM DAVIS

Ballantine Books • New York

A Ballantine Books Trade Paperback Original

Copyright © 2008 by PAWS, Inc. All Rights Reserved.
"GARFIELD" and the GARFIELD characters are registered and unregistered trademarks of PAWS, Inc.

Published in the United States by Ballantine Books, an imprint of The Random House Publishing Group,
a division of Random House, Inc., New York.

BALLANTINE and colophon are registered trademarks of Random House, Inc.

ISBN 978-0-345-51387-8

Printed in the United States of America

www.ballantinebooks.com

9 8 7 6 5 4 3 2 1

741.5973
DAV
11/08

CONTENTS

Foreword by Dan Walsh

WHAT IS MY PURPOSE IN LIFE?

When I was a kid, I loved Garfield. Gathered in my little bedroom was a pretty impressive collection of books, toys, and posters. Like many children of my generation, I wanted to be just like Garfield— lazy, sarcastic, lasagna loving, Monday hating, cynical but under it all, a darn good guy. And I did a pretty good job, apart from the lasagna bit; we were more about the potatoes in my lovely Irish household.

Inevitably I became a teenager, and I realized that while it was definitely fun to be just like Garfield, well, girls just didn't seem to go for lazy, sarcastic, lasagna-loving, Monday-hating, cynical guys. I guess Garfield had the same problem. So for a while my Garfield fascination took a little rest while I chased girls, grew my hair long, wore far too many earrings, and bought my first guitar.

The years passed, and somehow I never became a rock star, I never made it into *Rolling Stone* magazine, or *The New York Times*, or *The Washington Post*, or *Time* magazine. Heck, it got so bad that I actually had to get myself a regular job. With a tie. And a haircut! What was going on with the world?! How could this be?!

Pretty soon I was working hard every day, coming home and waiting for the phone to ring. I'd sit around my apartment, finding more and more ingenious ways to entertain myself without blowing my paycheck: watching bad movies, drinking lots of coffee, making catastrophic attempts at calling girls for dates (don't even go there), and playing my guitar when no one wanted to listen (it was almost as if it was some kind of badly tuned accordion . . .). In fact, my life was very, very similar to a certain Mr. Jon Arbuckle's: Jon Arbuckle was kind of lonely, disheartened, crazy, disillusioned, and, well, just like me.

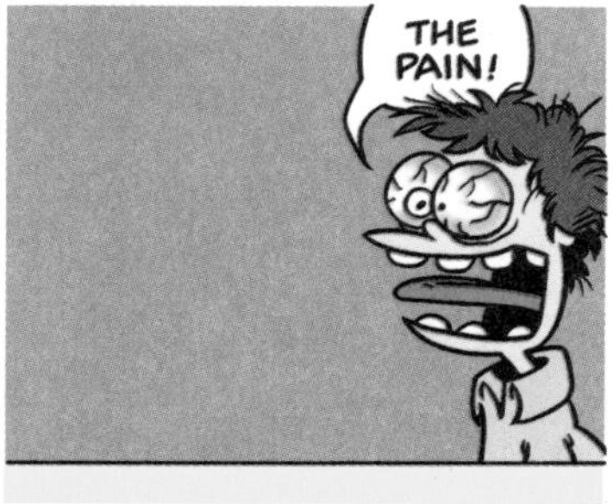
THE PAIN!

Jon played by the rules. He worked hard, he was kind to his neighbors, he put in some effort to impress the ladies (come on, those suits, the plaid, the yellows, the vibrant reds, the, um, gorilla costumes, ten out of ten for effort I say), and yet, where was the payoff? Why were we at home alone watching bad movies on the weekends? When was something fun and exciting going to happen in our lives? Why did our hair look so bad? Where did our goldfish keep disappearing to? In fact, I discovered that if Garfield wasn't in the strip at all, then Jon and I were like kindred spirits. Constantly lamenting the passing of our youth, pondering all those missed opportunities, wondering if we'd ever get a date, crying into our cereal (come on, it was a Monday), putting socks on our heads for fun. . . .

I started to remove the cat from the strip sometime around the beginning of 2008 and found it a curiously fascinating and compelling experience. The results were both absolutely hilarious and instantly recognizable. I wasn't just looking and laughing at Jon's existential angst, I was laughing at myself and my family and my friends.

Soon I found I just couldn't stop myself; it was like scratching dozens of those lottery scratch cards every day and winning every time. Some of the results made me think, some made me sad, some made me titter, and some made me laugh until tears streamed down my face. It was so totally and utterly and perfectly hilariously depressing!

The funny thing is Jon has always been talking to himself. Garfield never *really* answers because his replies are always just thoughts. Have a look. It's true! Jon has always been telling us these things; it's just that with Garfield there you've been getting distracted from the truth: Jon needs some help!

When I first began erasing Garfield from the comics and posting them on garfieldminusgarfield.net, I thought a few of my friends might get a laugh from it. It seemed pretty funny to me (having said that — just like Jon — I'm a pretty odd person), and I was sure my friends would get the joke, too. So every day I'd post a few strips and a few people would visit. Then something strange and

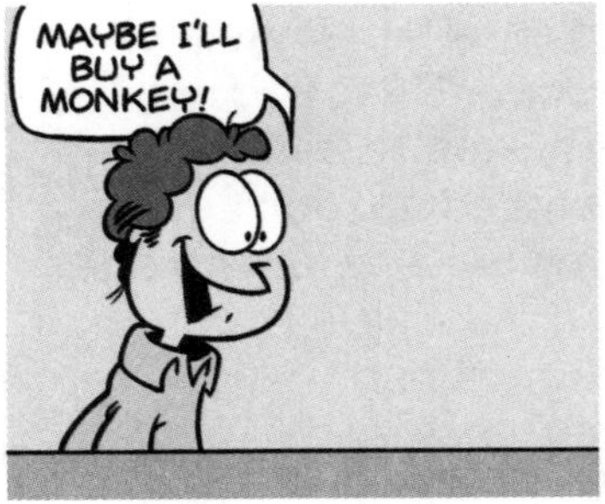
MAYBE I'LL BUY A MONKEY!

slightly scary happened: One day 1,500 people visited the site. "Okay," I thought, "no reason to panic. Jim Davis probably wasn't one of them; tomorrow things will go back to normal." However, the next day 15,000 people visited, the next 50,000, then 100,000, then 200,000, then *half a million a day*!

It's difficult to get across just how exciting and absolutely terrifying the Garfield Minus Garfield explosion was. Most days I was as nervous as a fern in Garfield's hungry path. But some good friends gave me advice and support and I kept the site running, thinking any day Jim Davis would send that inevitable cease-and-desist order. In the meantime the fan mail started arriving, and I began to find out firsthand just how much people identified with Jon: "It's like looking in a mirror," "He reminds me so much of myself," and even "Thank you. My post-teenage angst and disquietude has never quite felt so at ease with a comic."

Without a doubt the most heartwarming fan mails I received were from people suffering with bipolar depression. Of all the fan mail that arrived, these were the most appreciative and touching. One said:

> *I just wanted to write and say that your strip is genius. I think that it is very special and portrays suburban isolation due to bipolar/depression/mental illness so accurately that it's almost scary. I have been dealing with bipolar and depression for the past five years and am just now coming out of a three-year period of Jon Arbuckle's frighteningly similar lonely and sad existence. Some of the strips portray EXACTLY some of the thoughts and feelings and actions I had over that period of time. Just wanted you to know and keep up the good work!*

Go Jon!

It was around this time that magic things started to happen. As Garfield Minus Garfield's popularity grew, it attracted the attention of the mainstream media. One particularly charming and persuasive journalist convinced me to provide an interview and reveal my identity — I agreed on provision that she check with her lawyers what they thought of the strip.

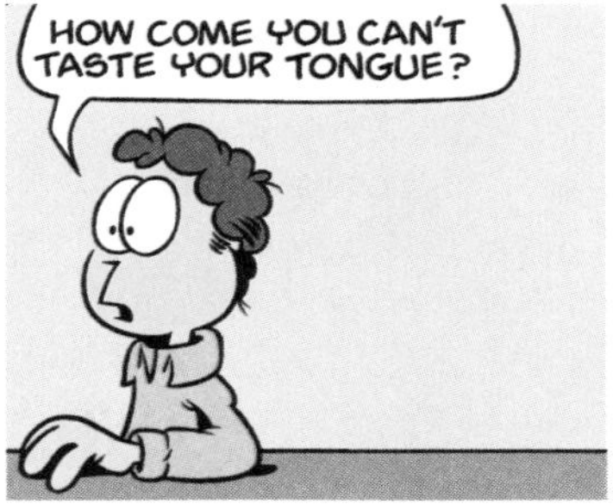
HOW COME YOU CAN'T TASTE YOUR TONGUE?

Well, instead of doing that, this particular journalist asked Jim Davis what he thought of the strip. Oh dear! As it turned out Jim was an occasional visitor to the site, and he called it "an inspired thing to do." He then went on to thank me for enabling him to see another side of Garfield.

Well.

I can promise you I'm not exaggerating when I say that I floated. I absolutely and positively floated with happiness. I floated to work, I floated home, I floated for every waking moment, and in fact I'm still floating now.

Over the course of the following weeks and months I was interviewed and Garfield Minus Garfield was reviewed in many publications, including (you guessed it): *Rolling Stone* magazine, *The New York Times*, *The Washington Post,* and *Time* magazine (the Dalai Lama was on the front page, Jon and I were near the back, I guess that's okay). Jon took me on a trip to all the places I've always wanted to go to, and he's still doing it, every day.

Now, thanks to the awesome generosity and humor of Jim Davis, Garfield Minus Garfield is a book, and I'm absolutely honored to be part of it.

I'd just like to say thanks to Jim Davis and Jon Arbuckle for bringing a little bit of magic and a lot of laughs into my life, and hopefully, within the pages of this book, they will do the same thing for you, too.

Dan Walsh
July 23, 2008

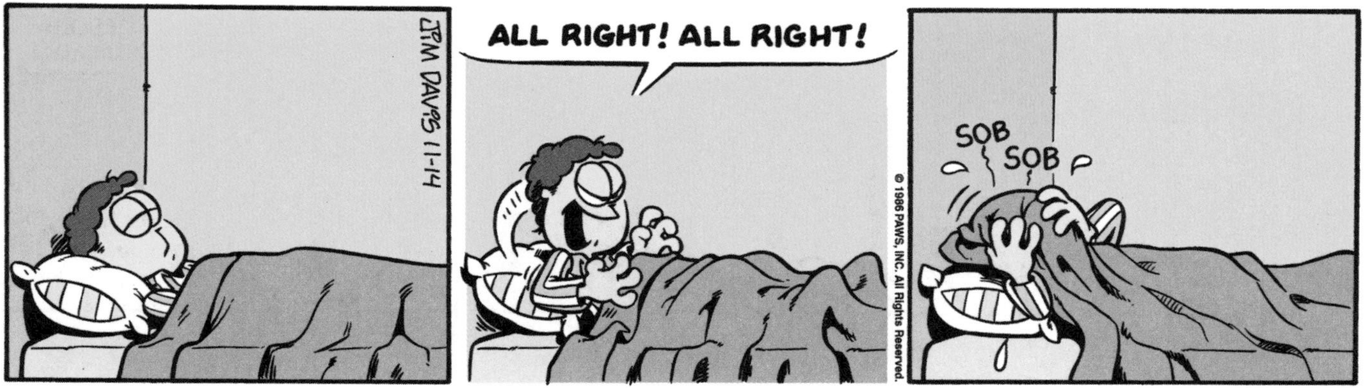
JIM DAVIS 11-14
ALL RIGHT! ALL RIGHT!
© 1986 PAWS, INC. All Rights Reserved.
SOB
SOB

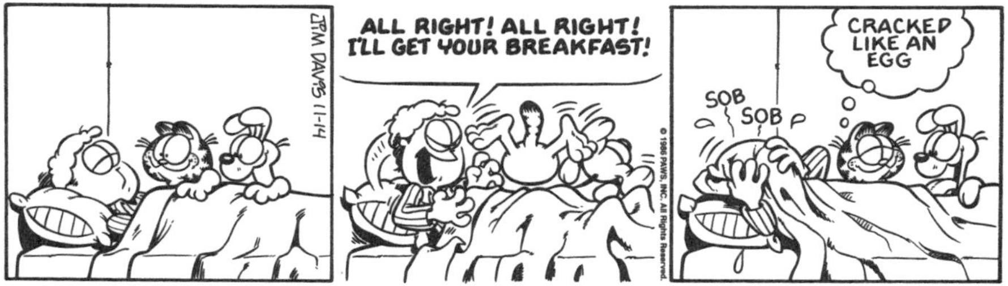
JIM DAVIS 11-14
ALL RIGHT! ALL RIGHT! I'LL GET YOUR BREAKFAST!
SOB
SOB
CRACKED LIKE AN EGG

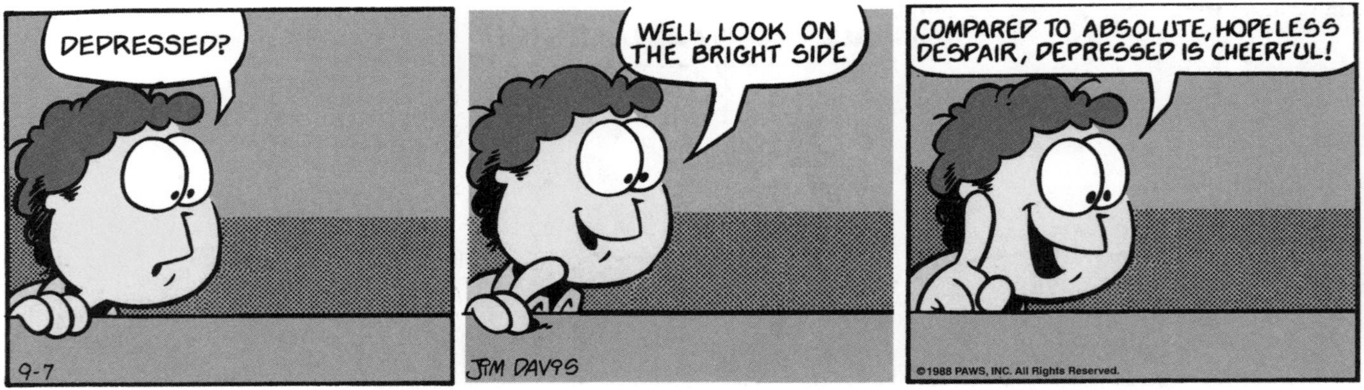
DEPRESSED?
WELL, LOOK ON THE BRIGHT SIDE
COMPARED TO ABSOLUTE, HOPELESS DESPAIR, DEPRESSED IS CHEERFUL!
9-7
JIM DAVIS
©1988 PAWS, INC. All Rights Reserved.

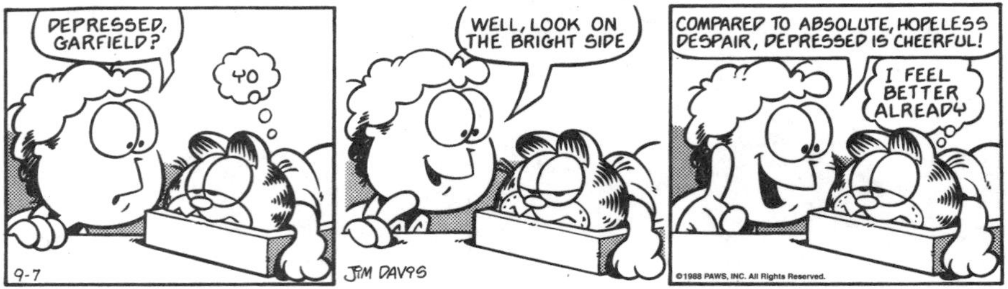
DEPRESSED, GARFIELD?
YO
WELL, LOOK ON THE BRIGHT SIDE
COMPARED TO ABSOLUTE, HOPELESS DESPAIR, DEPRESSED IS CHEERFUL!
I FEEL BETTER ALREADY
9-7
JIM DAVIS
©1988 PAWS, INC. All Rights Reserved.

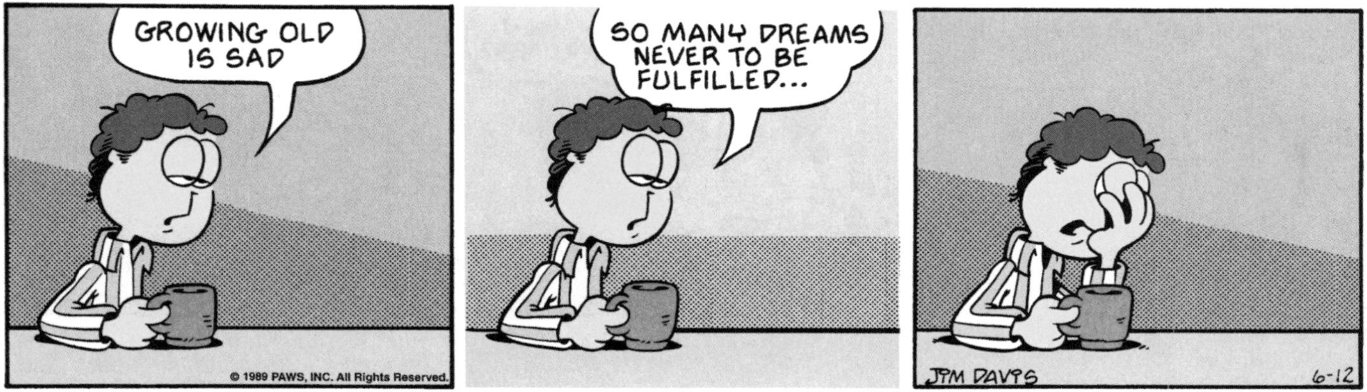
GROWING OLD IS SAD
© 1989 PAWS, INC. All Rights Reserved.
SO MANY DREAMS NEVER TO BE FULFILLED...
JIM DAVIS
6-12

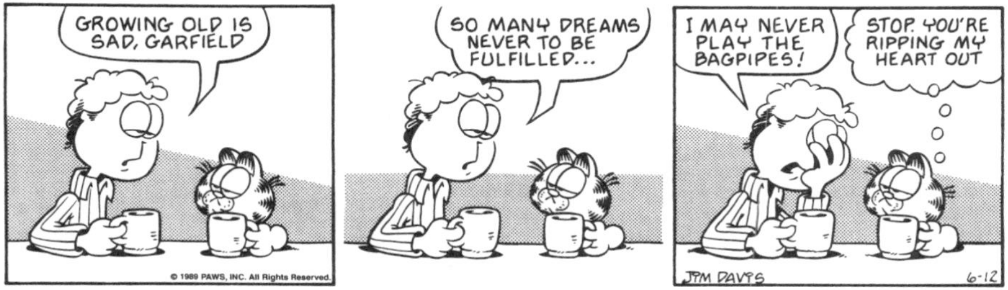
GROWING OLD IS SAD, GARFIELD
© 1989 PAWS, INC. All Rights Reserved.
SO MANY DREAMS NEVER TO BE FULFILLED...
I MAY NEVER PLAY THE BAGPIPES!
STOP. YOU'RE RIPPING MY HEART OUT
JIM DAVIS
6-12

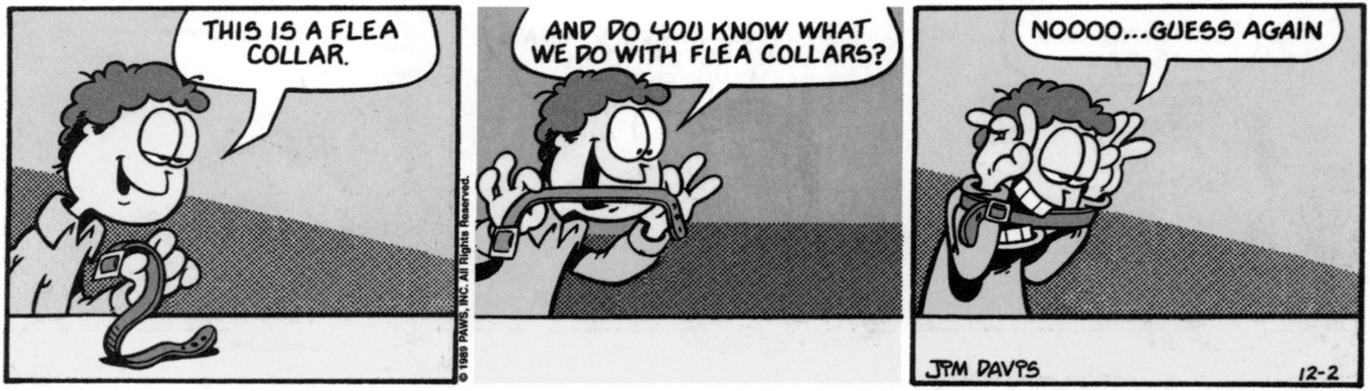
THIS IS A FLEA COLLAR.
© 1989 PAWS, INC. All Rights Reserved.
AND DO YOU KNOW WHAT WE DO WITH FLEA COLLARS?
NOOOO...GUESS AGAIN
JIM DAVIS
12-2

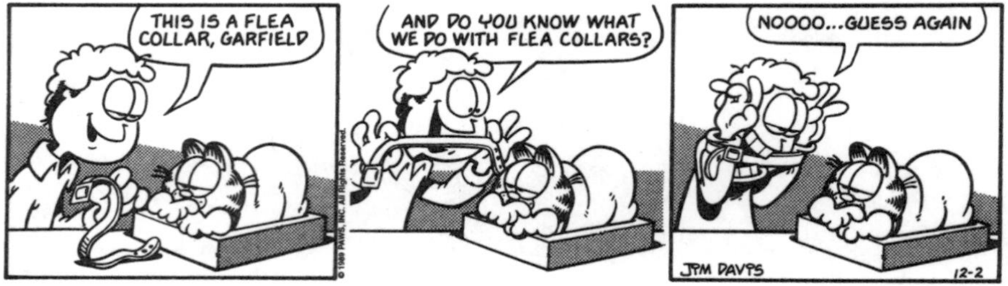
THIS IS A FLEA COLLAR, GARFIELD
AND DO YOU KNOW WHAT WE DO WITH FLEA COLLARS?
NOOOO...GUESS AGAIN
JIM DAVIS
12-2

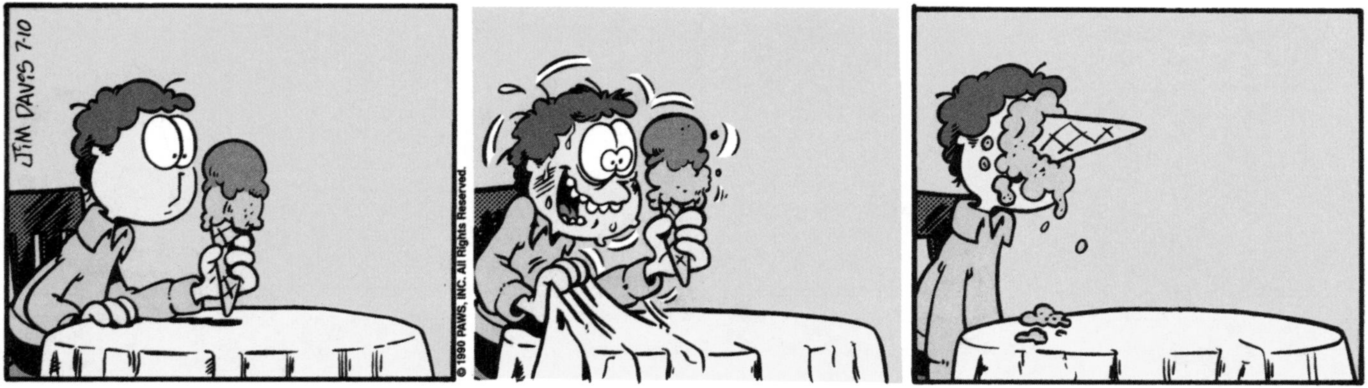
JIM DAVIS 7-10
© 1990 PAWS, INC. All Rights Reserved.

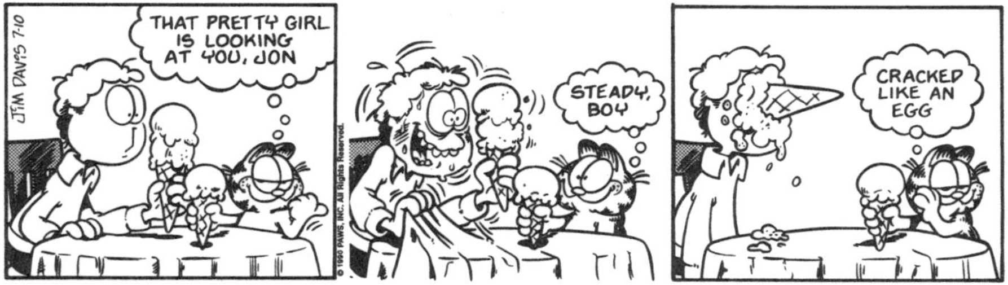
JIM DAVIS 7-10
THAT PRETTY GIRL IS LOOKING AT YOU, JON
© 1990 PAWS, INC. All Rights Reserved.
STEADY, BOY
CRACKED LIKE AN EGG

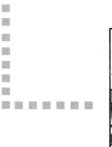

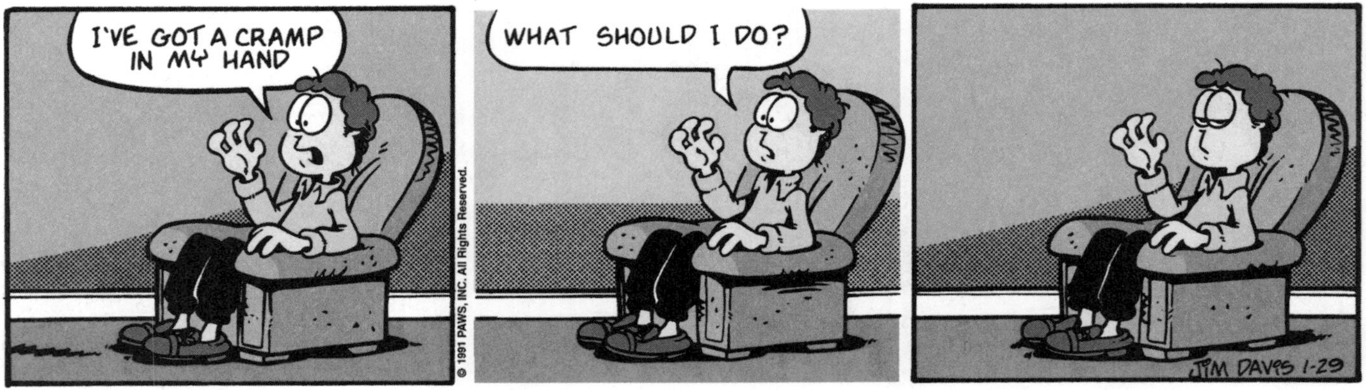
I'VE GOT A CRAMP IN MY HAND
© 1991 PAWS, INC. All Rights Reserved.
WHAT SHOULD I DO?
JIM DAVIS 1-29

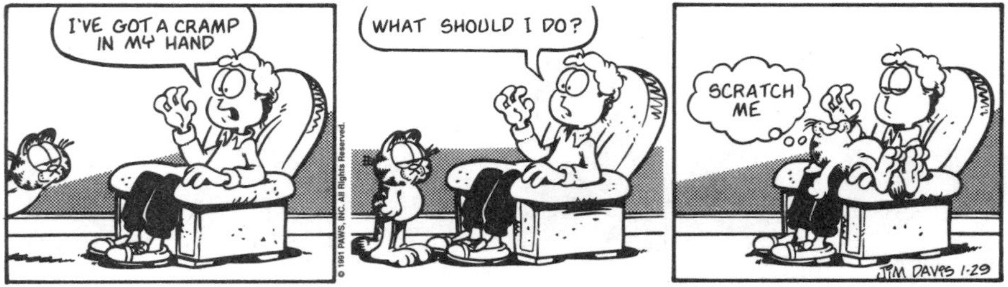
I'VE GOT A CRAMP IN MY HAND
© 1991 PAWS, INC. All Rights Reserved.
WHAT SHOULD I DO?
SCRATCH ME
JIM DAVIS 1-29

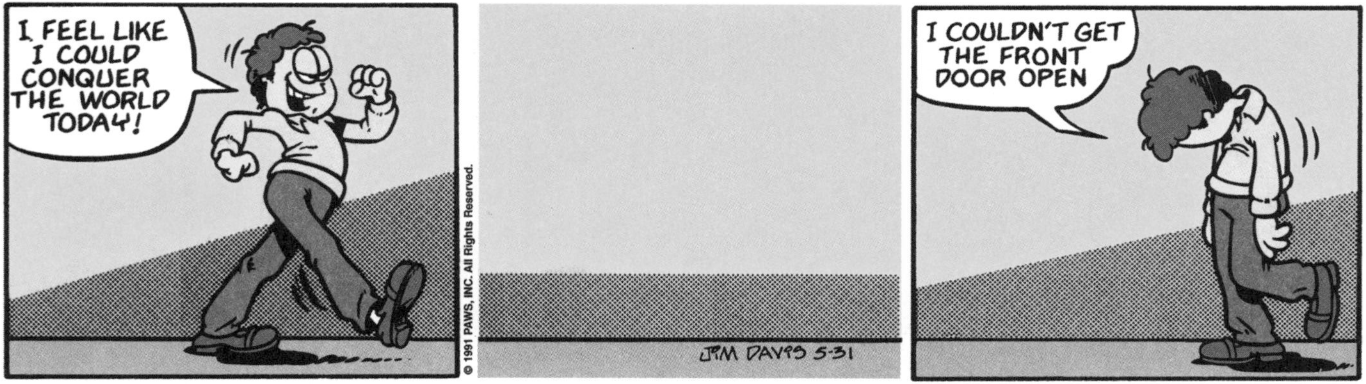
I FEEL LIKE I COULD CONQUER THE WORLD TODAY!
© 1991 PAWS, INC. All Rights Reserved.
JIM DAVIS 5-31
I COULDN'T GET THE FRONT DOOR OPEN

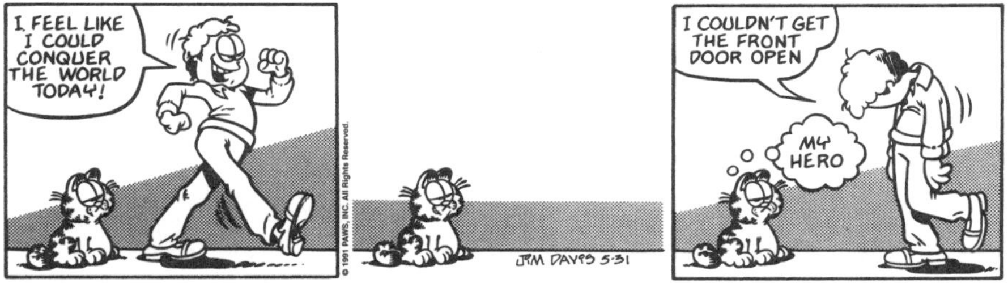
I FEEL LIKE I COULD CONQUER THE WORLD TODAY!
© 1991 PAWS, INC. All Rights Reserved.
JIM DAVIS 5-31
I COULDN'T GET THE FRONT DOOR OPEN
MY HERO

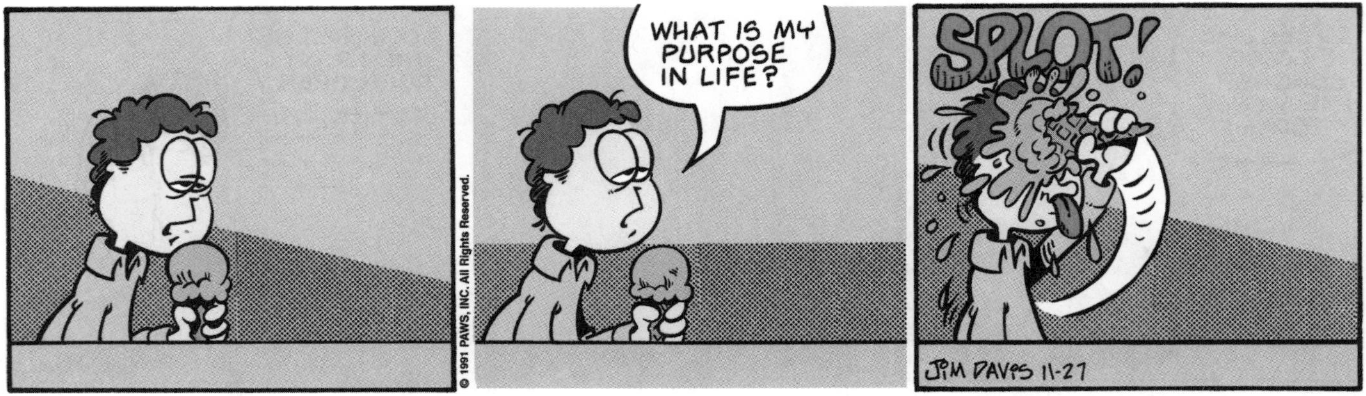
WHAT IS MY PURPOSE IN LIFE?
SPLOT!
© 1991 PAWS, INC. All Rights Reserved.
JIM DAVIS 11-27

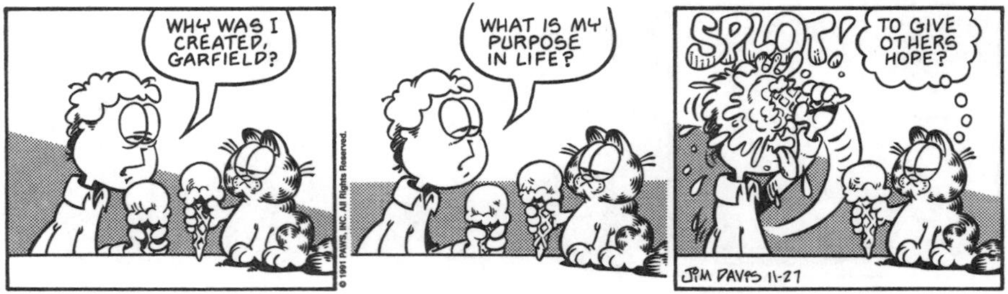
WHY WAS I CREATED, GARFIELD?
WHAT IS MY PURPOSE IN LIFE?
SPLOT!
TO GIVE OTHERS HOPE?
© 1991 PAWS, INC. All Rights Reserved.
JIM DAVIS 11-27

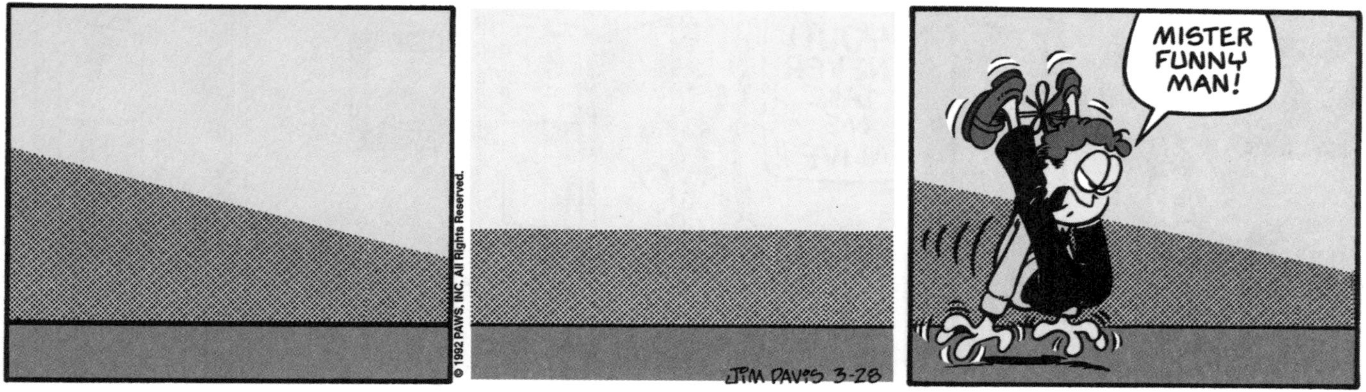
© 1992 PAWS, INC. All Rights Reserved.
JIM DAVIS 3-28
MISTER FUNNY MAN!

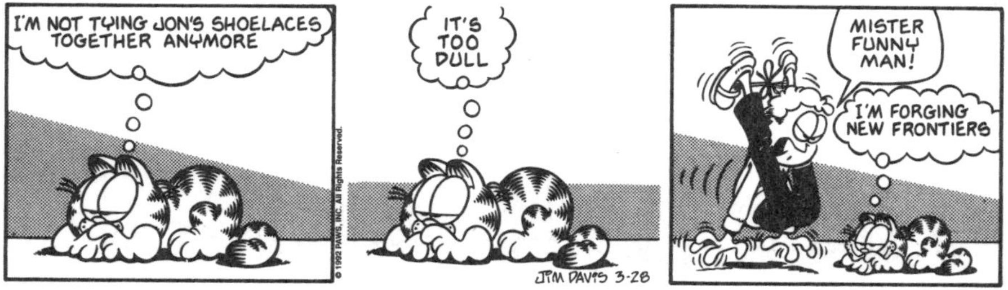
I'M NOT TYING JON'S SHOELACES TOGETHER ANYMORE
© 1992 PAWS, INC. All Rights Reserved.
IT'S TOO DULL
JIM DAVIS 3-28
MISTER FUNNY MAN!
I'M FORGING NEW FRONTIERS

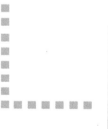

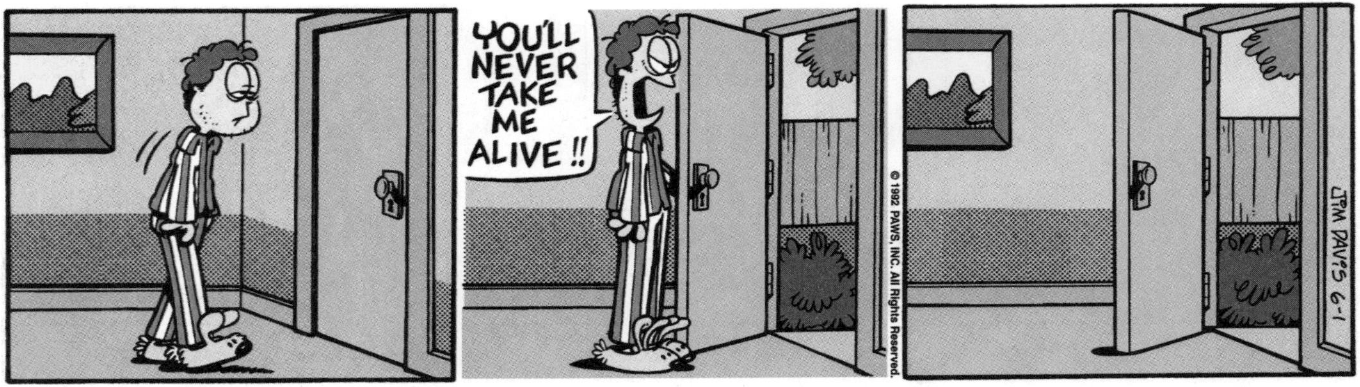
YOU'LL NEVER TAKE ME ALIVE !!
© 1992 PAWS, INC. All Rights Reserved.
JIM DAVIS 6-1

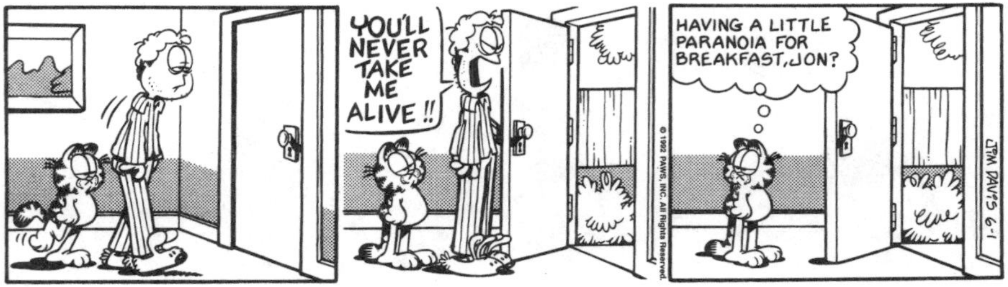
YOU'LL NEVER TAKE ME ALIVE !!
© 1992 PAWS, INC. All Rights Reserved.
HAVING A LITTLE PARANOIA FOR BREAKFAST, JON?
JIM DAVIS 6-1

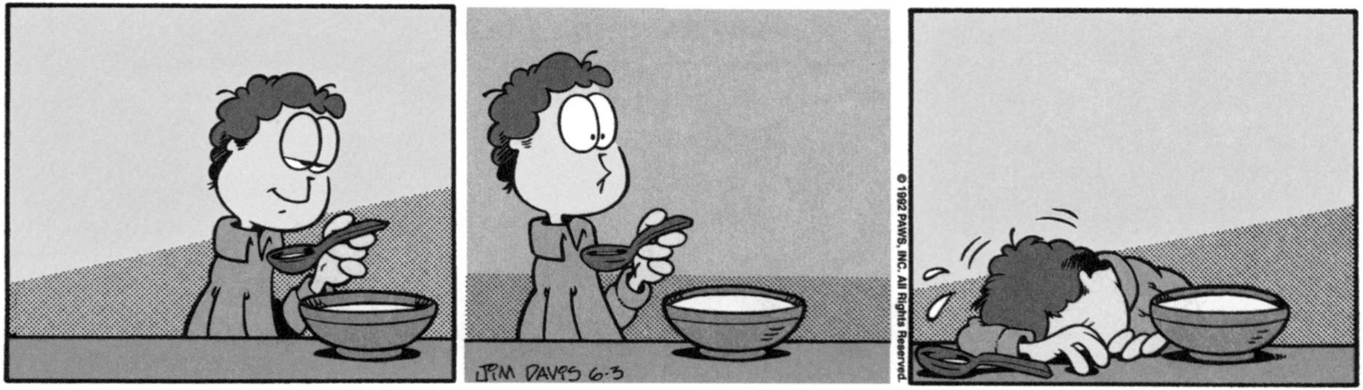
JIM DAVIS 6-3
© 1992 PAWS, INC. All Rights Reserved.

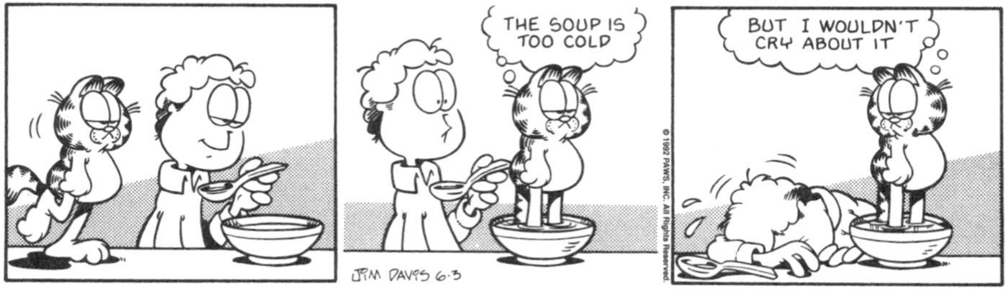
THE SOUP IS TOO COLD
BUT I WOULDN'T CRY ABOUT IT
JIM DAVIS 6-3

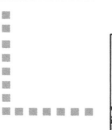

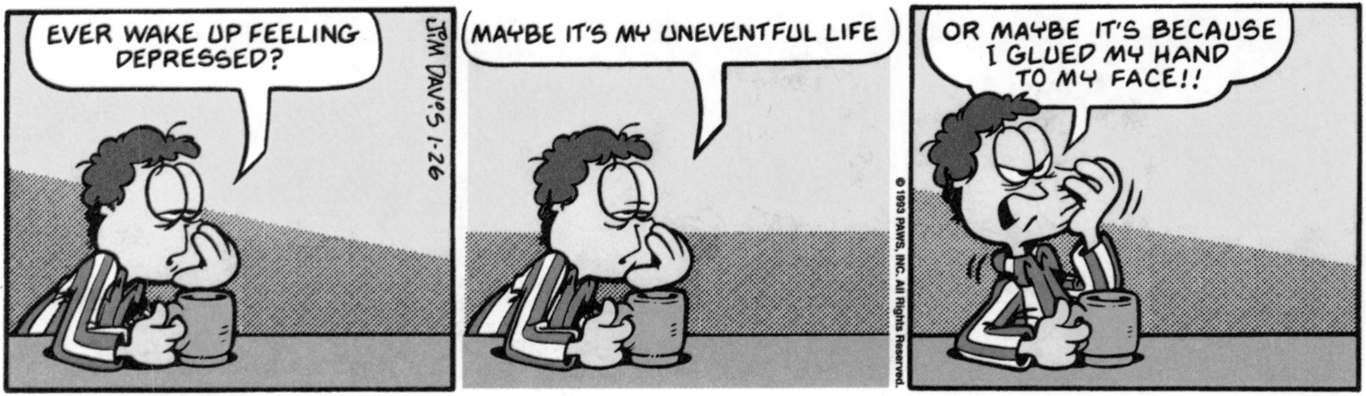
EVER WAKE UP FEELING DEPRESSED?
JIM DAVIS 1-26
MAYBE IT'S MY UNEVENTFUL LIFE
© 1993 PAWS, INC. All Rights Reserved.
OR MAYBE IT'S BECAUSE I GLUED MY HAND TO MY FACE!!

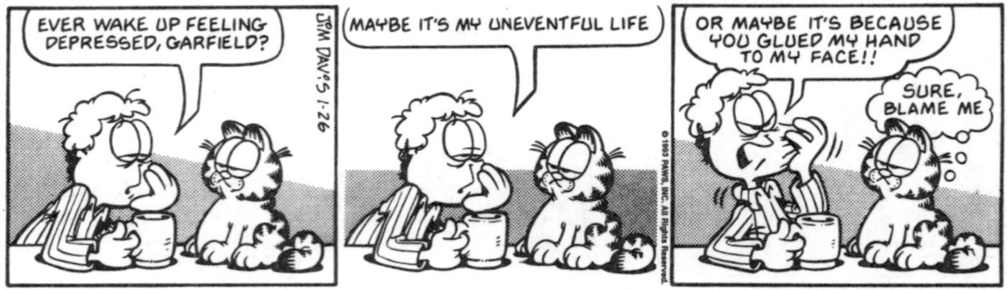
EVER WAKE UP FEELING DEPRESSED, GARFIELD?
JIM DAVIS 1-26
MAYBE IT'S MY UNEVENTFUL LIFE
OR MAYBE IT'S BECAUSE YOU GLUED MY HAND TO MY FACE!!
SURE, BLAME ME

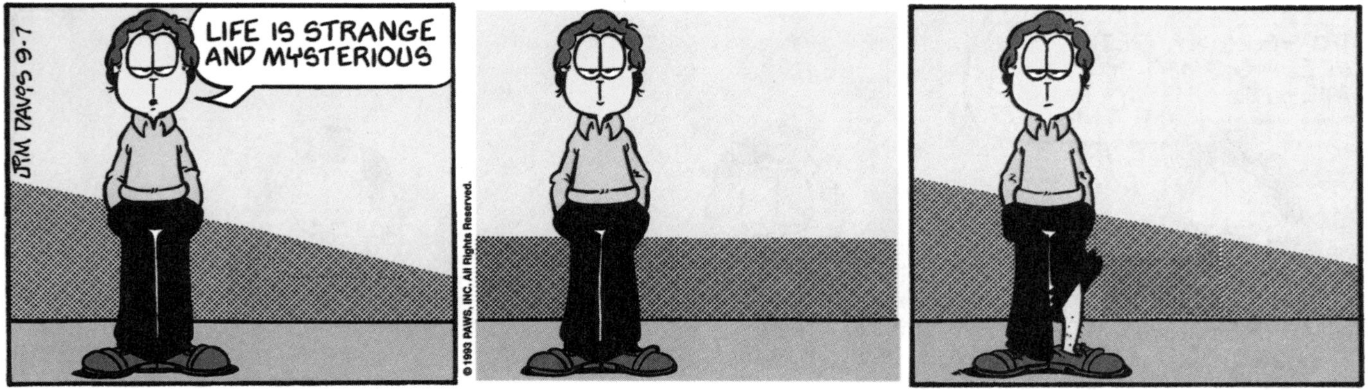
JIM DAVIS 9-7
LIFE IS STRANGE AND MYSTERIOUS
© 1993 PAWS, INC. All Rights Reserved.

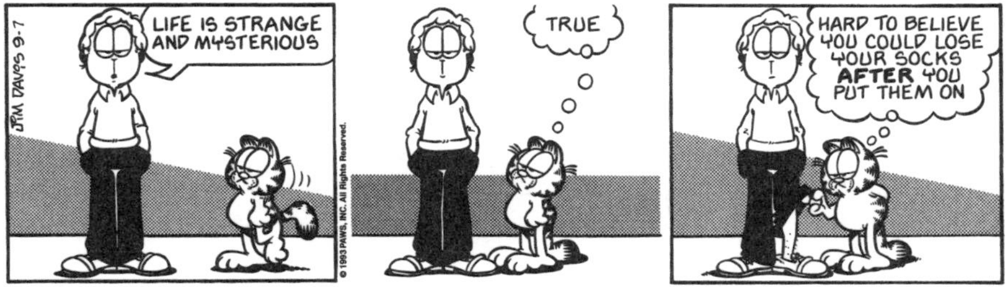
JIM DAVIS 9-7
LIFE IS STRANGE AND MYSTERIOUS
© 1993 PAWS, INC. All Rights Reserved.
TRUE
HARD TO BELIEVE YOU COULD LOSE YOUR SOCKS **AFTER** YOU PUT THEM ON

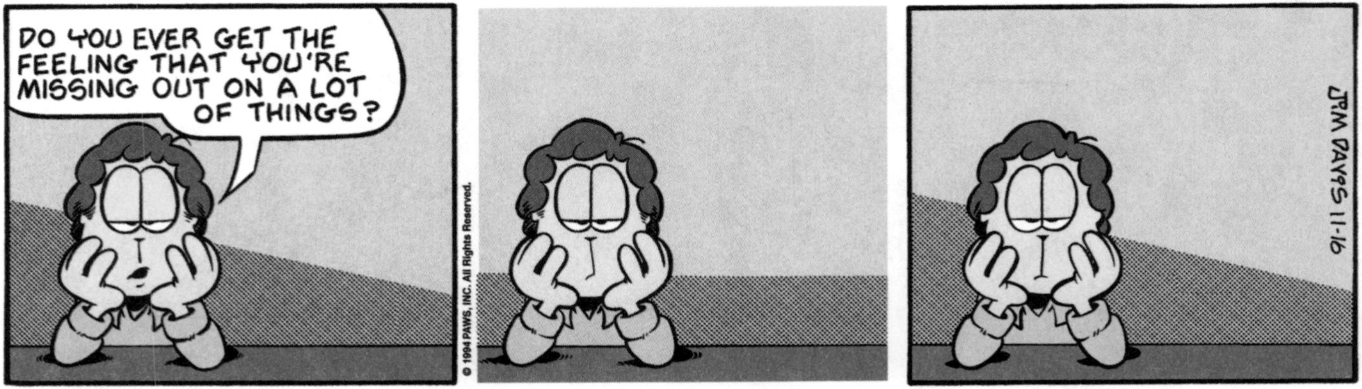
DO YOU EVER GET THE FEELING THAT YOU'RE MISSING OUT ON A LOT OF THINGS?
© 1994 PAWS, INC. All Rights Reserved.
JIM DAVIS 11-16

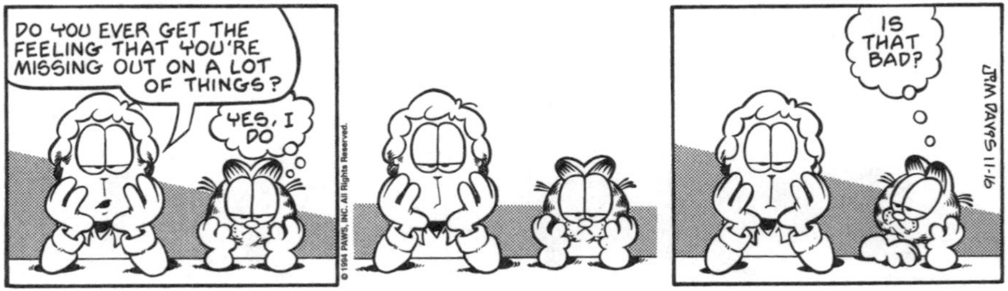
DO YOU EVER GET THE FEELING THAT YOU'RE MISSING OUT ON A LOT OF THINGS?
YES, I DO
© 1994 PAWS, INC. All Rights Reserved.
IS THAT BAD?
JIM DAVIS 11-16

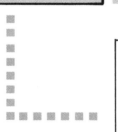

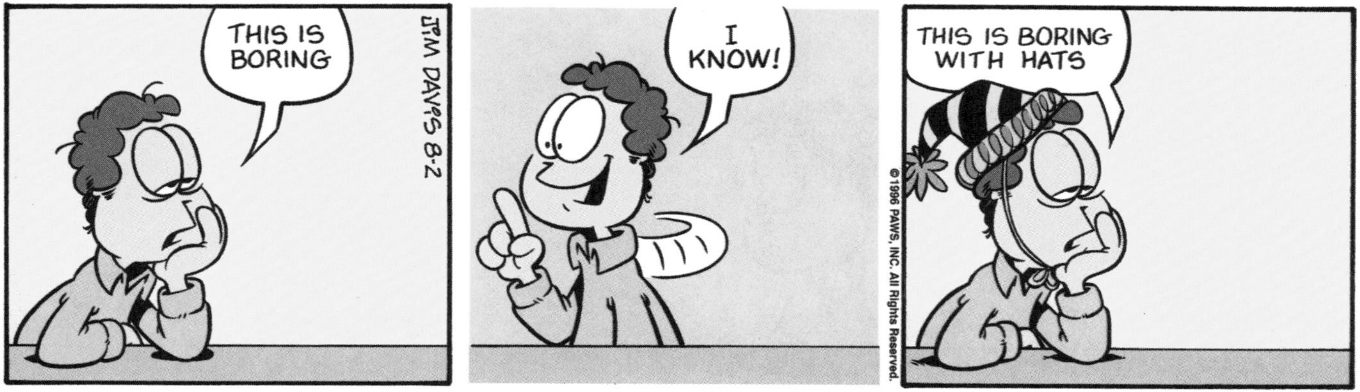
THIS IS BORING
JIM DAVIS 8-2
I KNOW!
© 1996 PAWS, INC. All Rights Reserved.
THIS IS BORING WITH HATS

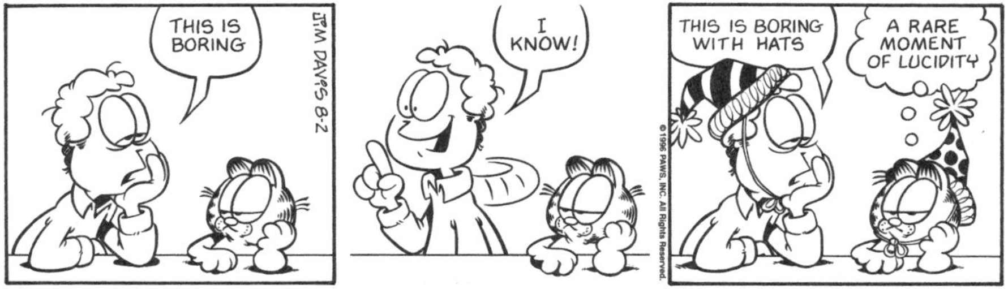
THIS IS BORING
JIM DAVIS 8-2
I KNOW!
© 1996 PAWS, INC. All Rights Reserved.
THIS IS BORING WITH HATS
A RARE MOMENT OF LUCIDITY

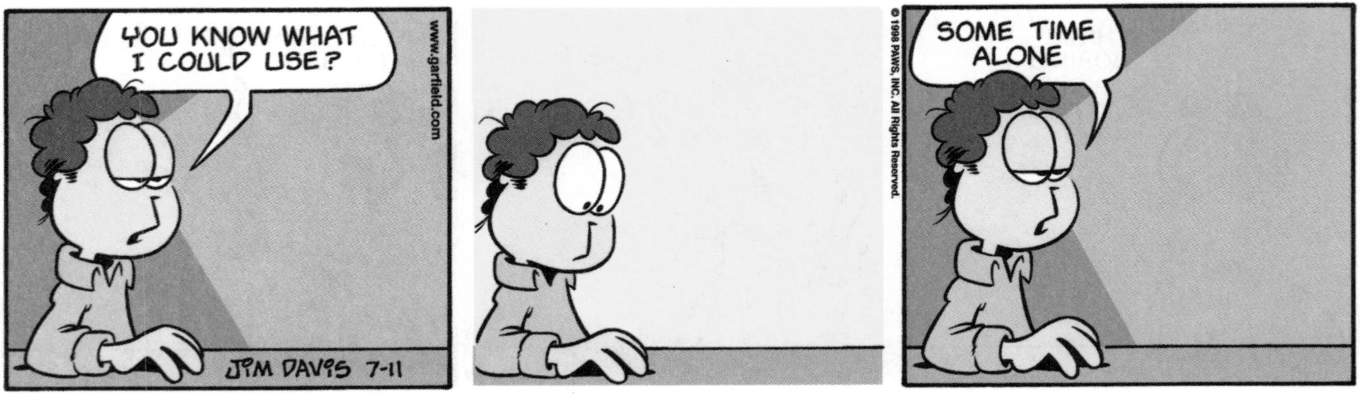
YOU KNOW WHAT I COULD USE?
www.garfield.com
JIM DAVIS 7-11
© 1998 PAWS, INC. All Rights Reserved.
SOME TIME ALONE

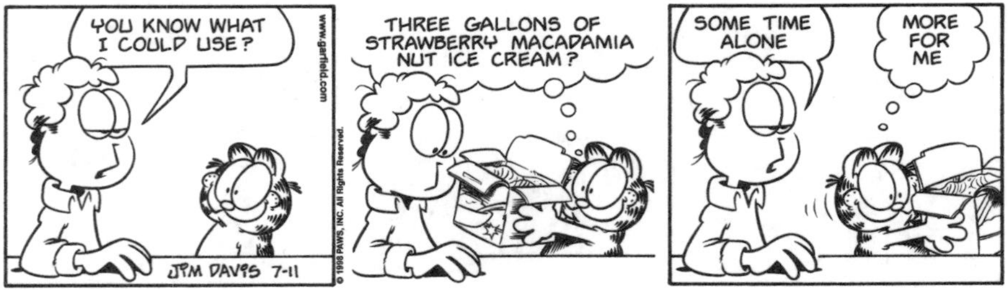
YOU KNOW WHAT I COULD USE?
www.garfield.com
JIM DAVIS 7-11
© 1998 PAWS, INC. All Rights Reserved.
THREE GALLONS OF STRAWBERRY MACADAMIA NUT ICE CREAM?
SOME TIME ALONE
MORE FOR ME

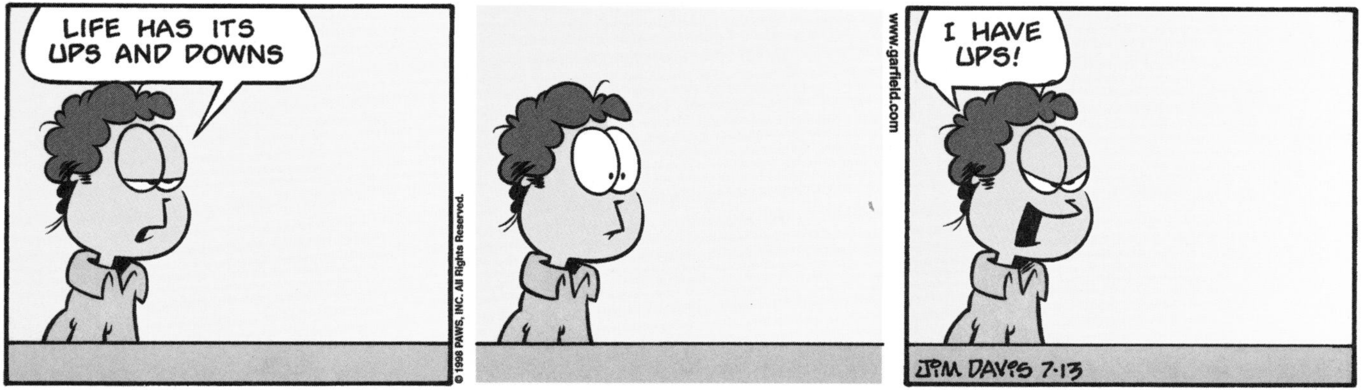
LIFE HAS ITS UPS AND DOWNS
© 1998 PAWS, INC. All Rights Reserved.
www.garfield.com
I HAVE UPS!
JIM DAVIS 7-13

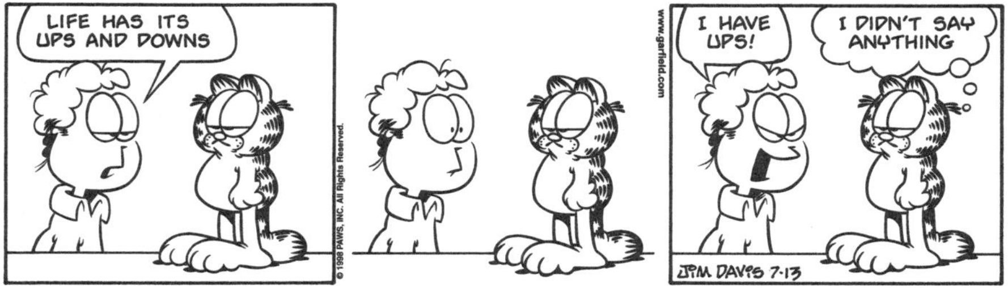
LIFE HAS ITS UPS AND DOWNS
© 1998 PAWS, INC. All Rights Reserved.
www.garfield.com
I HAVE UPS!
I DIDN'T SAY ANYTHING
JIM DAVIS 7-13

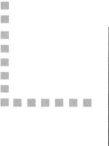

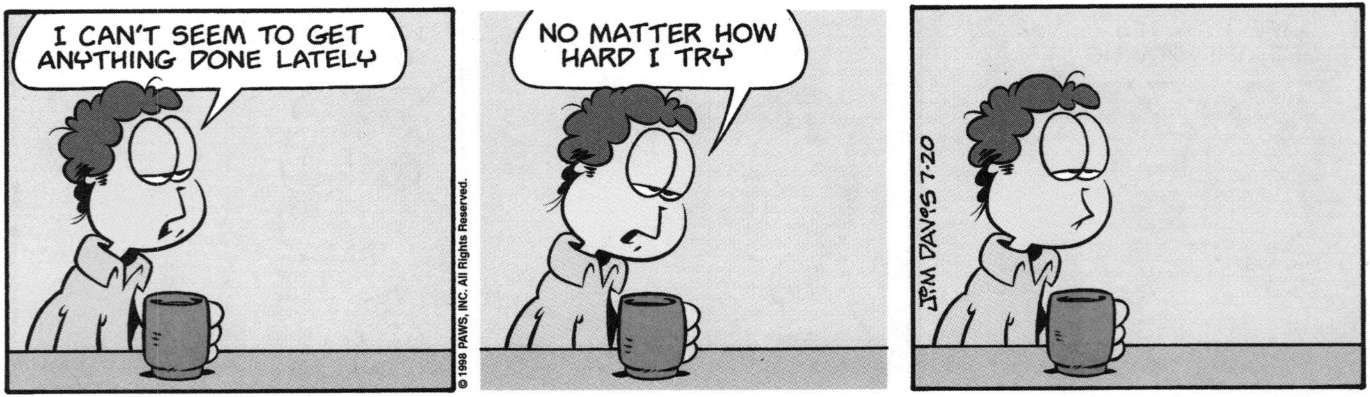
I CAN'T SEEM TO GET ANYTHING DONE LATELY
NO MATTER HOW HARD I TRY
© 1998 PAWS, INC. All Rights Reserved.

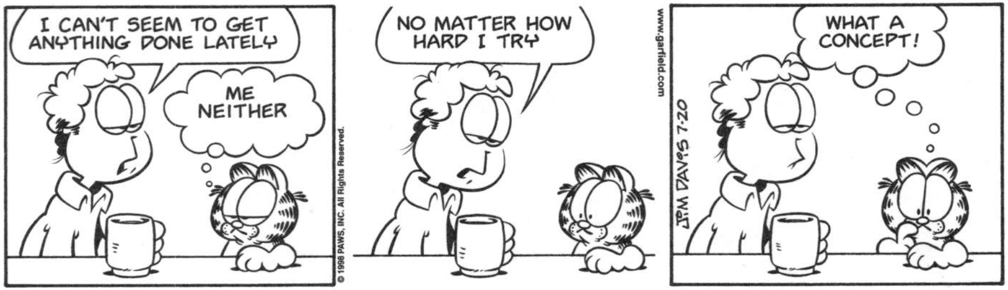
I CAN'T SEEM TO GET ANYTHING DONE LATELY
ME NEITHER
NO MATTER HOW HARD I TRY
WHAT A CONCEPT!
© 1998 PAWS, INC. All Rights Reserved.
www.garfield.com

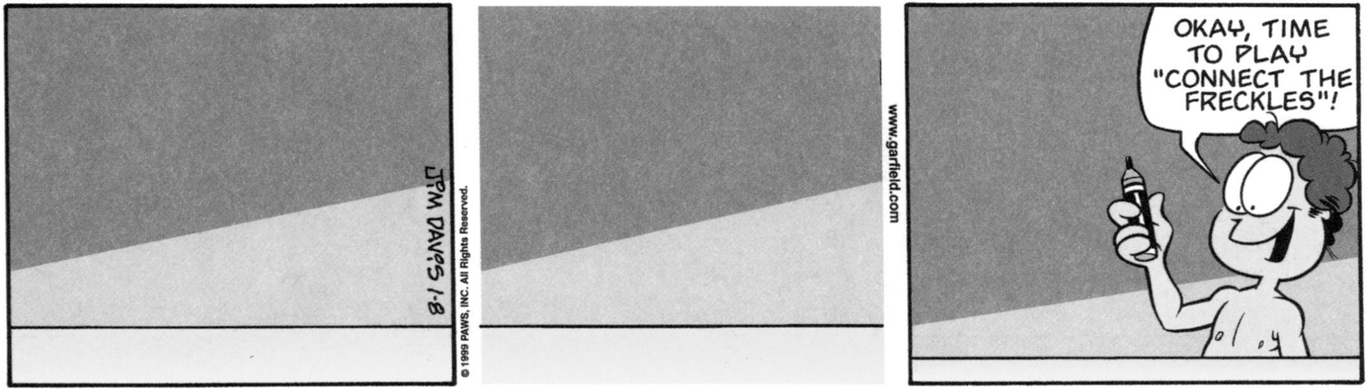

JPM DAVIS 1-8
© 1999 PAWS, INC. All Rights Reserved.
www.garfield.com
OKAY, TIME TO PLAY "CONNECT THE FRECKLES"!

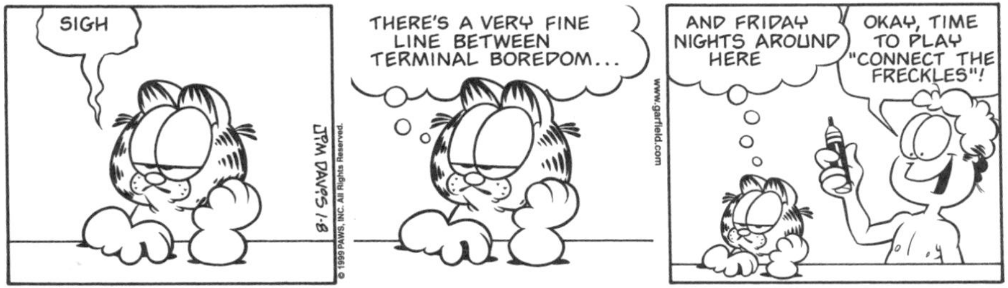

SIGH
JPM DAVIS 1-8
© 1999 PAWS, INC. All Rights Reserved.
THERE'S A VERY FINE LINE BETWEEN TERMINAL BOREDOM...
www.garfield.com
AND FRIDAY NIGHTS AROUND HERE
OKAY, TIME TO PLAY "CONNECT THE FRECKLES"!

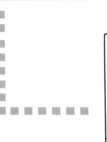

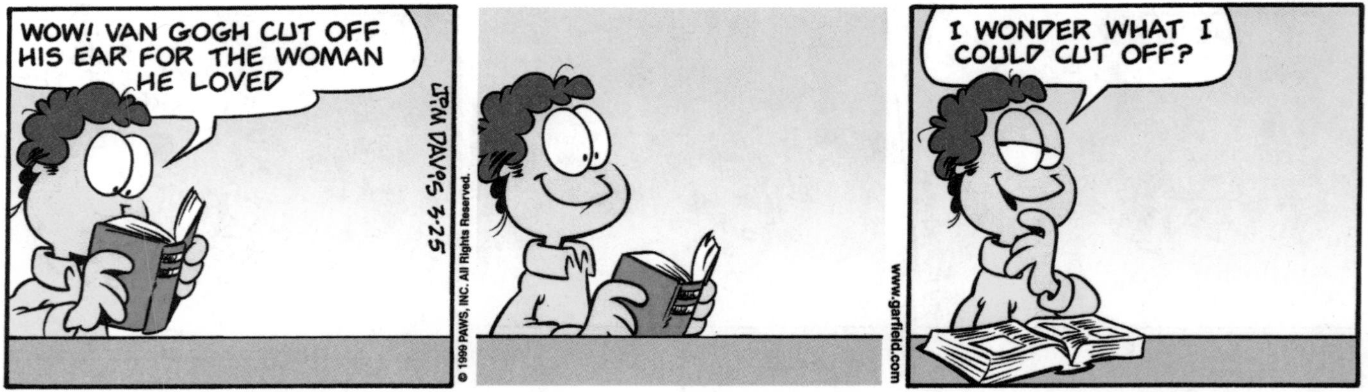
WOW! VAN GOGH CUT OFF HIS EAR FOR THE WOMAN HE LOVED
JIM DAVIS 3-25
© 1999 PAWS, INC. All Rights Reserved.
I WONDER WHAT I COULD CUT OFF?
www.garfield.com

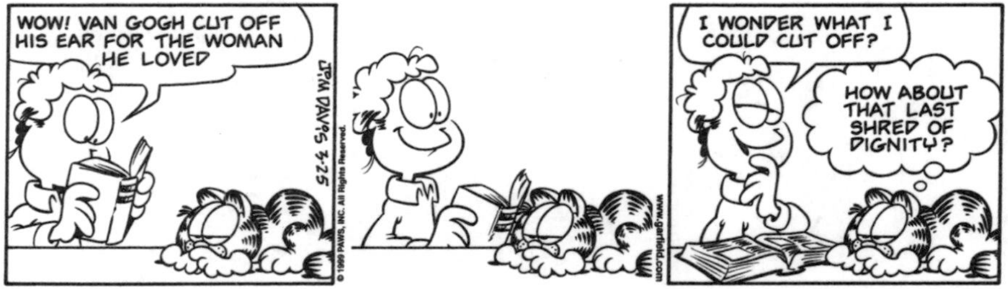
WOW! VAN GOGH CUT OFF HIS EAR FOR THE WOMAN HE LOVED
JIM DAVIS 3-25
© 1999 PAWS, INC. All Rights Reserved.
I WONDER WHAT I COULD CUT OFF?
HOW ABOUT THAT LAST SHRED OF DIGNITY?
www.garfield.com

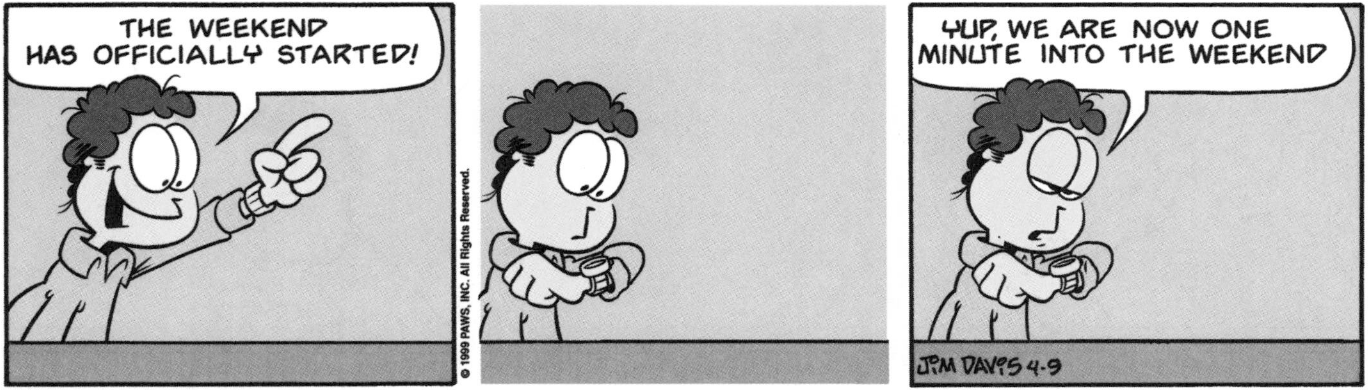
THE WEEKEND HAS OFFICIALLY STARTED!
© 1999 PAWS, INC. All Rights Reserved.
YUP, WE ARE NOW ONE MINUTE INTO THE WEEKEND
JIM DAVIS 4-9

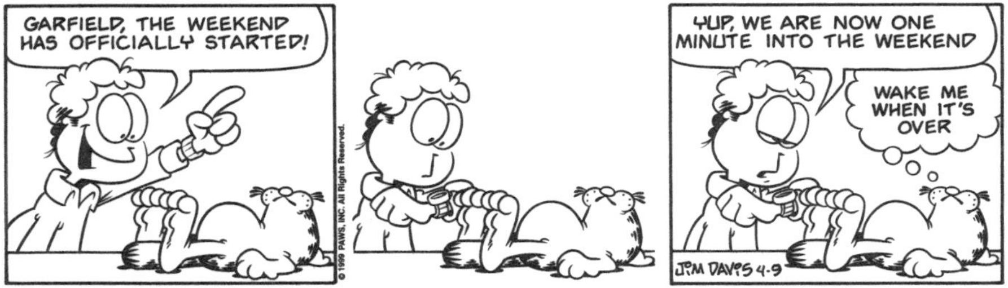
GARFIELD, THE WEEKEND HAS OFFICIALLY STARTED!
© 1999 PAWS, INC. All Rights Reserved.
YUP, WE ARE NOW ONE MINUTE INTO THE WEEKEND
WAKE ME WHEN IT'S OVER
JIM DAVIS 4-9

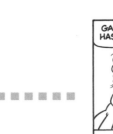

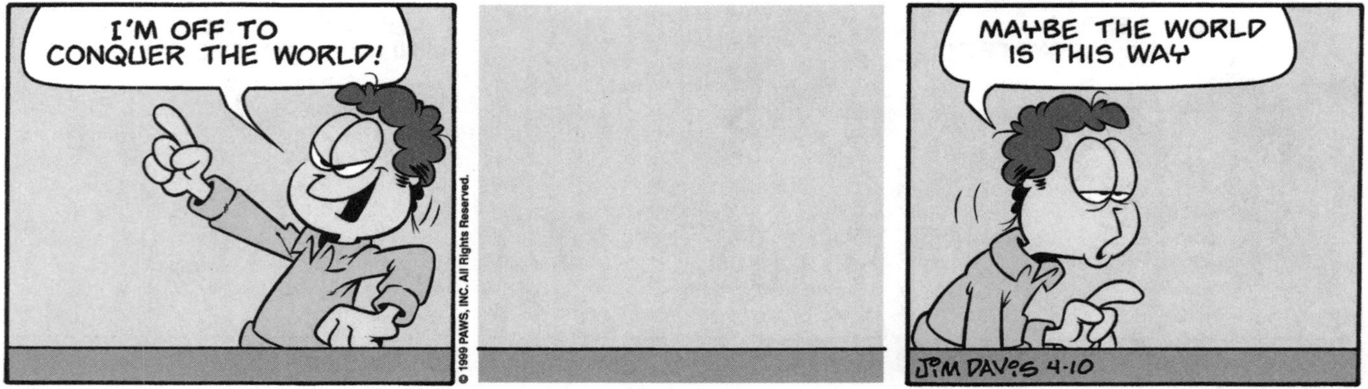
I'M OFF TO CONQUER THE WORLD!
© 1999 PAWS, INC. All Rights Reserved.
MAYBE THE WORLD IS THIS WAY
JIM DAVIS 4-10

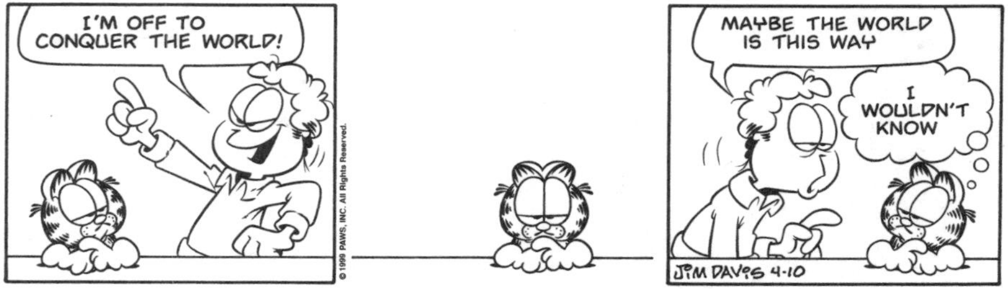
I'M OFF TO CONQUER THE WORLD!
© 1999 PAWS, INC. All Rights Reserved.
MAYBE THE WORLD IS THIS WAY
I WOULDN'T KNOW
JIM DAVIS 4-10

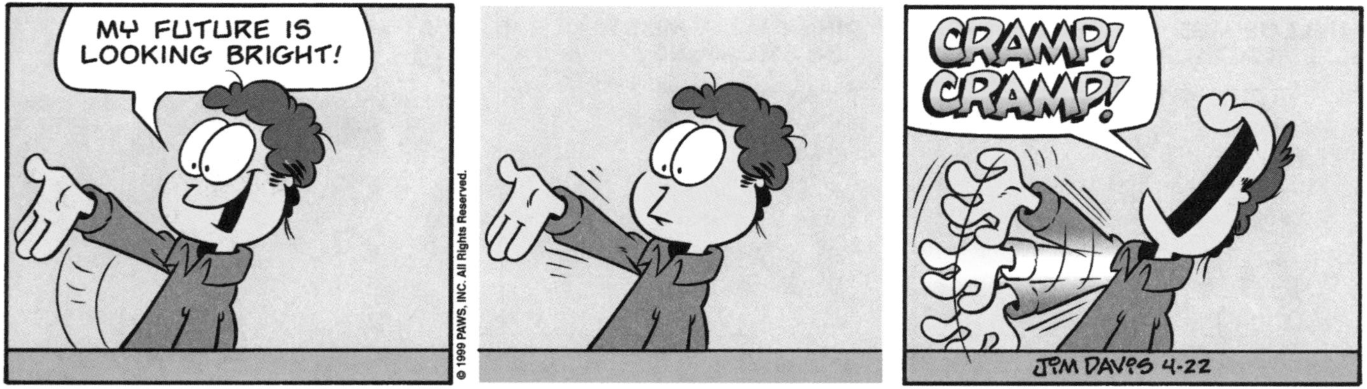
MY FUTURE IS LOOKING BRIGHT!
© 1999 PAWS, INC. All Rights Reserved.
CRAMP! CRAMP!
JIM DAVIS 4-22

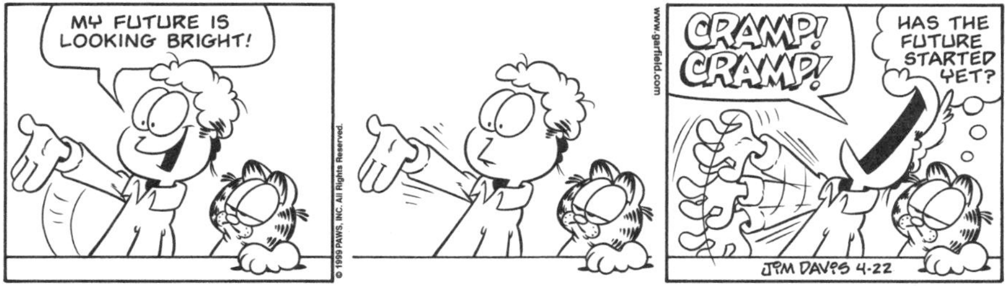
MY FUTURE IS LOOKING BRIGHT!
© 1999 PAWS, INC. All Rights Reserved.
www.garfield.com
CRAMP! CRAMP!
HAS THE FUTURE STARTED YET?
JIM DAVIS 4-22

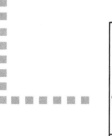

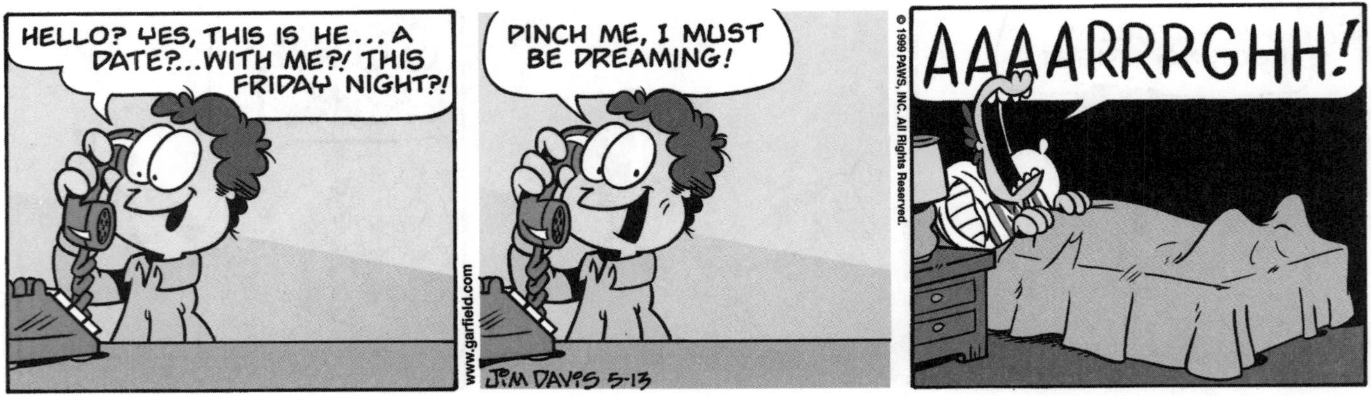
HELLO? YES, THIS IS HE... A DATE?...WITH ME?! THIS FRIDAY NIGHT?!
PINCH ME, I MUST BE DREAMING!
AAAARRRGHH!
www.garfield.com
JIM DAVIS 5-13
© 1999 PAWS, INC. All Rights Reserved.

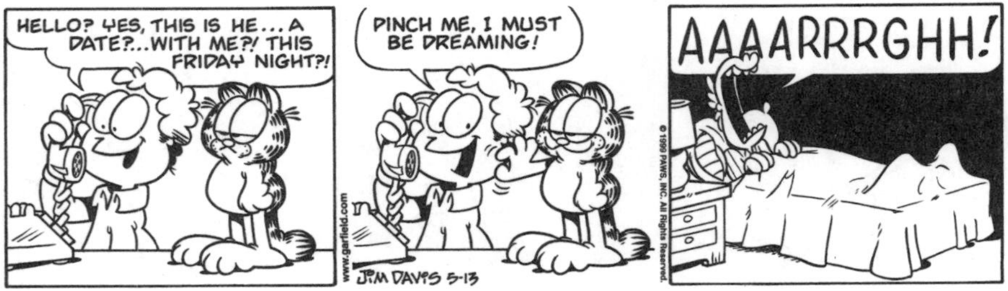
HELLO? YES, THIS IS HE... A DATE?...WITH ME?! THIS FRIDAY NIGHT?!
PINCH ME, I MUST BE DREAMING!
AAAARRRGHH!
www.garfield.com
JIM DAVIS 5-13
© 1999 PAWS, INC. All Rights Reserved.

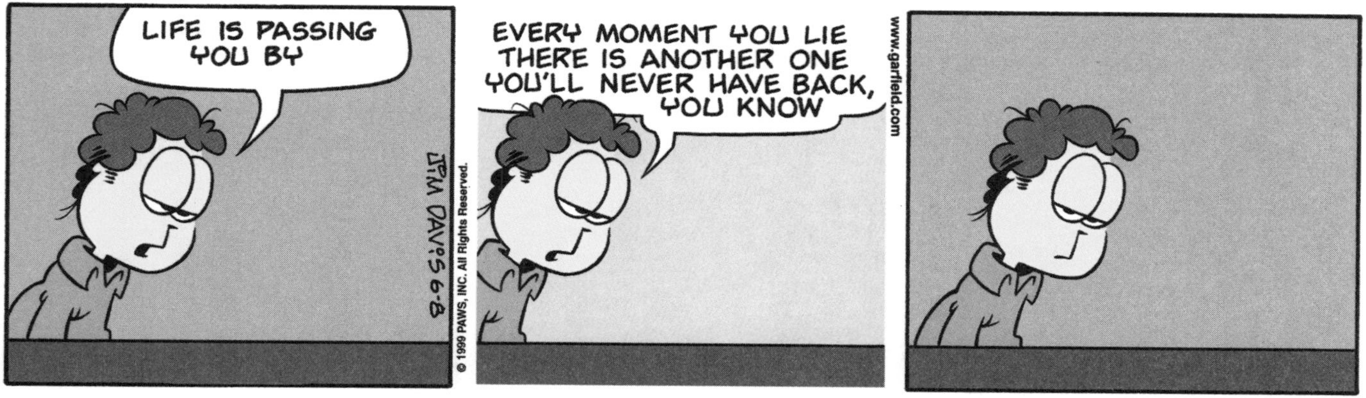
LIFE IS PASSING YOU BY
JIM DAVIS 6-8
© 1999 PAWS, INC. All Rights Reserved.
EVERY MOMENT YOU LIE THERE IS ANOTHER ONE YOU'LL NEVER HAVE BACK, YOU KNOW
www.garfield.com

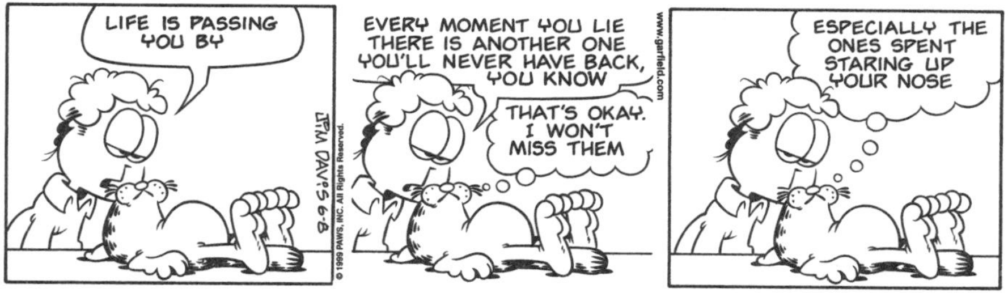
LIFE IS PASSING YOU BY
JIM DAVIS 6-8
© 1999 PAWS, INC. All Rights Reserved.
EVERY MOMENT YOU LIE THERE IS ANOTHER ONE YOU'LL NEVER HAVE BACK, YOU KNOW
THAT'S OKAY. I WON'T MISS THEM
www.garfield.com
ESPECIALLY THE ONES SPENT STARING UP YOUR NOSE

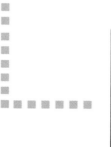

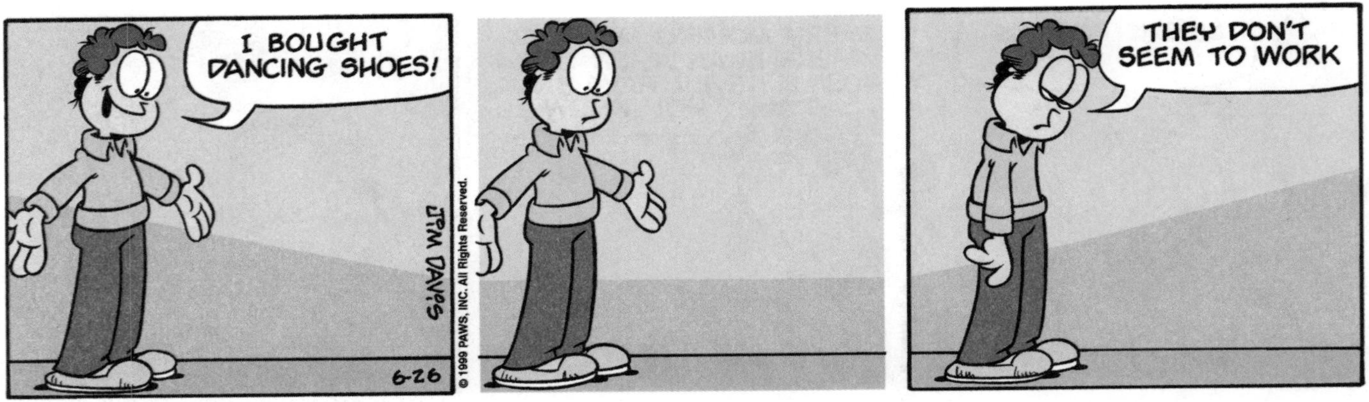
I BOUGHT DANCING SHOES!
JIM DAVIS
6-26
© 1999 PAWS, INC. All Rights Reserved.
THEY DON'T SEEM TO WORK

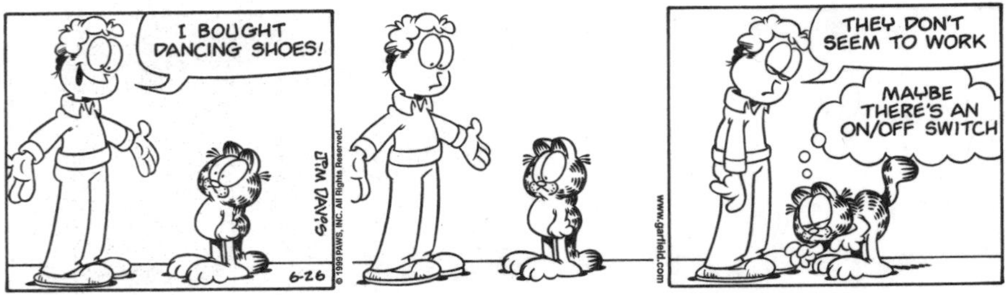
I BOUGHT DANCING SHOES!
JIM DAVIS
6-26
© 1999 PAWS, INC. All Rights Reserved.
www.garfield.com
THEY DON'T SEEM TO WORK
MAYBE THERE'S AN ON/OFF SWITCH

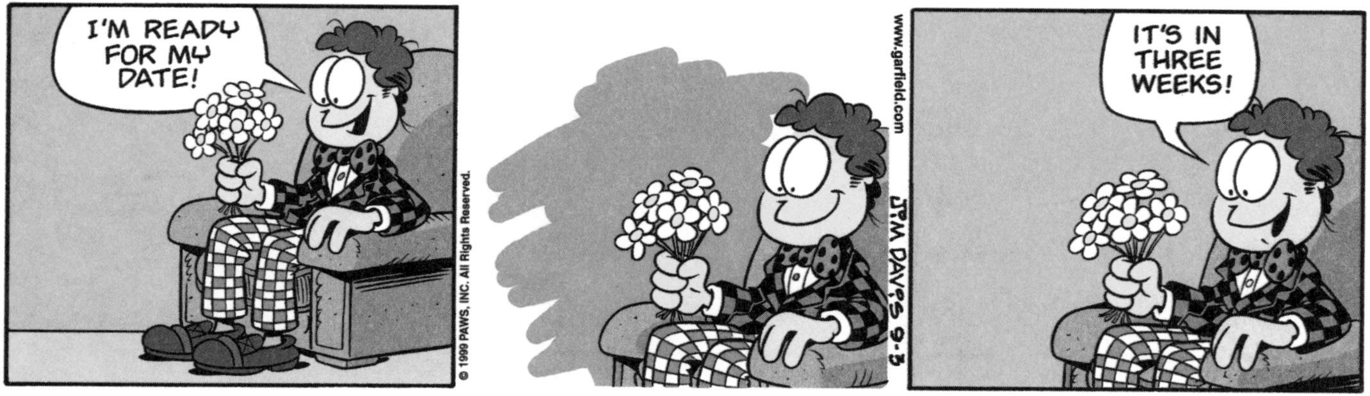
I'M READY FOR MY DATE!
© 1999 PAWS, INC. All Rights Reserved.
JIM DAVIS 9-3
www.garfield.com
IT'S IN THREE WEEKS!

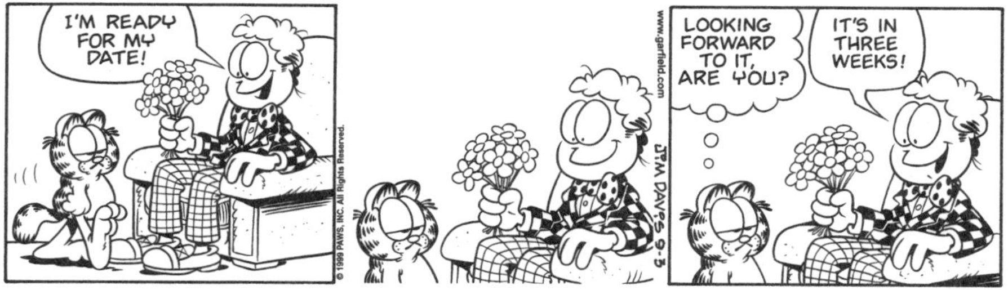
I'M READY FOR MY DATE!
© 1999 PAWS, INC. All Rights Reserved.
JIM DAVIS 9-3
www.garfield.com
IT'S IN THREE WEEKS!
LOOKING FORWARD TO IT, ARE YOU?

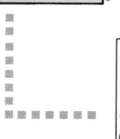

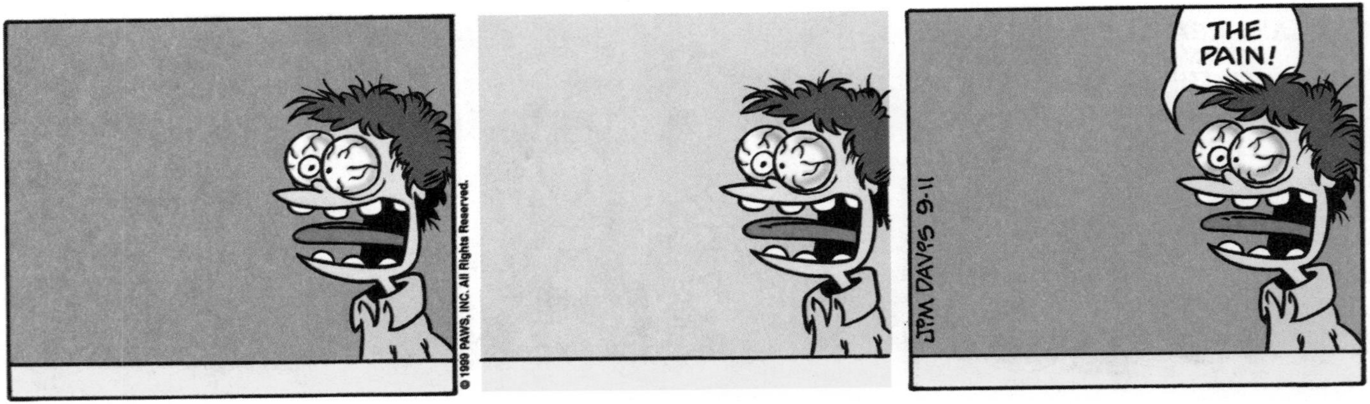
© 1999 PAWS, INC. All Rights Reserved.
THE PAIN!

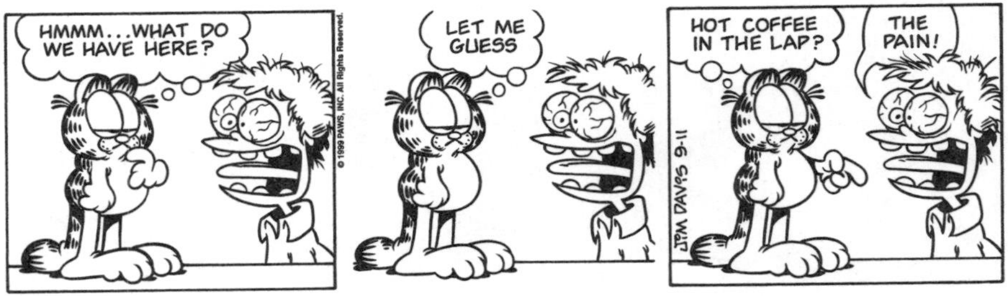
HMMM...WHAT DO WE HAVE HERE?
© 1999 PAWS, INC. All Rights Reserved.
LET ME GUESS
HOT COFFEE IN THE LAP?
THE PAIN!

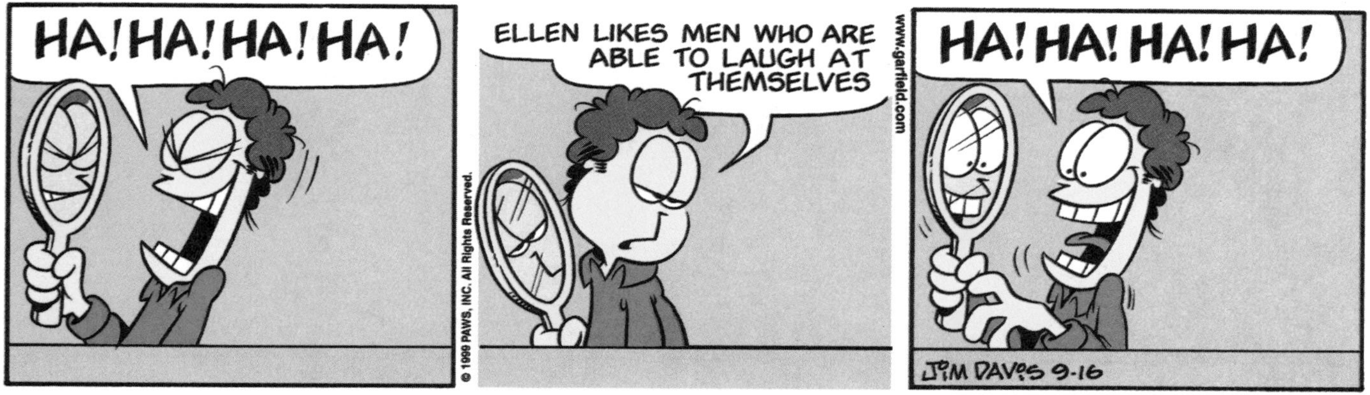
HA! HA! HA! HA!
© 1999 PAWS, INC. All Rights Reserved.
ELLEN LIKES MEN WHO ARE ABLE TO LAUGH AT THEMSELVES
www.garfield.com
HA! HA! HA! HA!
JIM DAVIS 9-16

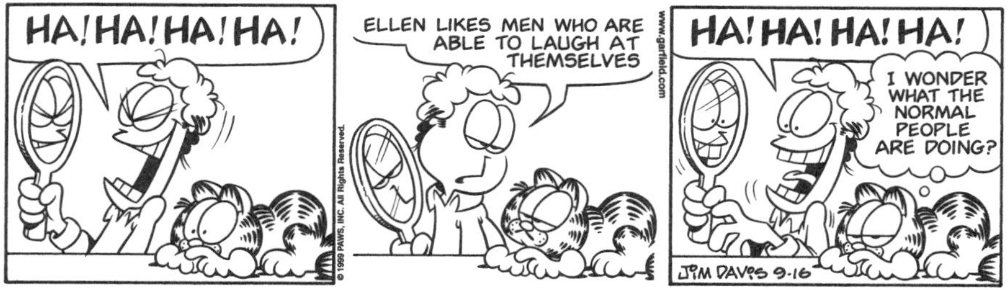
HA! HA! HA! HA!
© 1999 PAWS, INC. All Rights Reserved.
ELLEN LIKES MEN WHO ARE ABLE TO LAUGH AT THEMSELVES
www.garfield.com
HA! HA! HA! HA!
I WONDER WHAT THE NORMAL PEOPLE ARE DOING?
JIM DAVIS 9-16

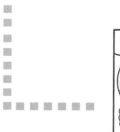

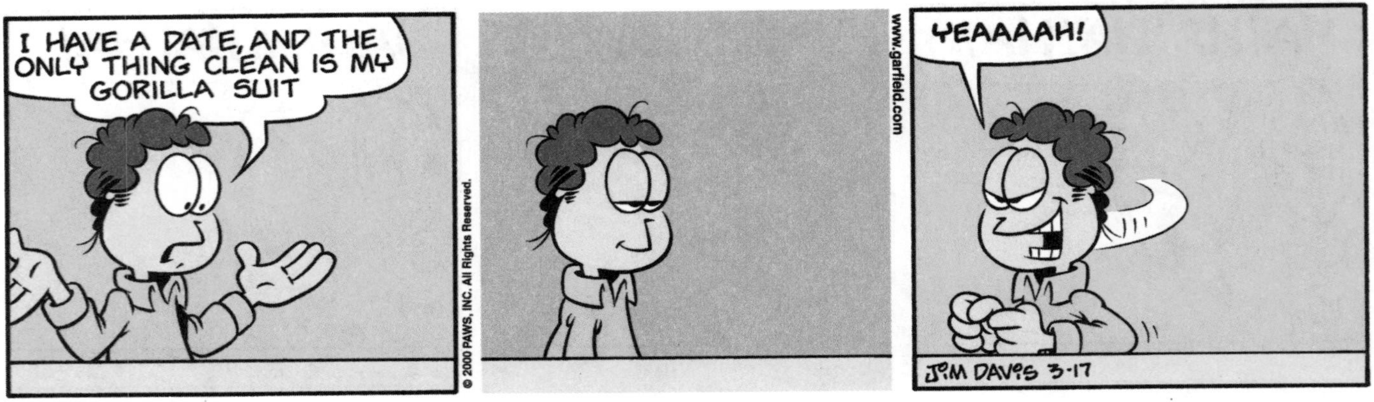
I HAVE A DATE, AND THE ONLY THING CLEAN IS MY GORILLA SUIT
© 2000 PAWS, INC. All Rights Reserved.
www.garfield.com
YEAAAAH!
JIM DAVIS 3-17

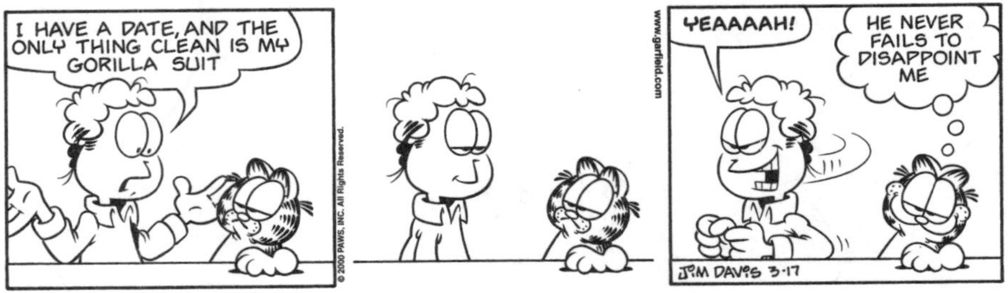
I HAVE A DATE, AND THE ONLY THING CLEAN IS MY GORILLA SUIT
© 2000 PAWS, INC. All Rights Reserved.
www.garfield.com
YEAAAAH!
HE NEVER FAILS TO DISAPPOINT ME
JIM DAVIS 3-17

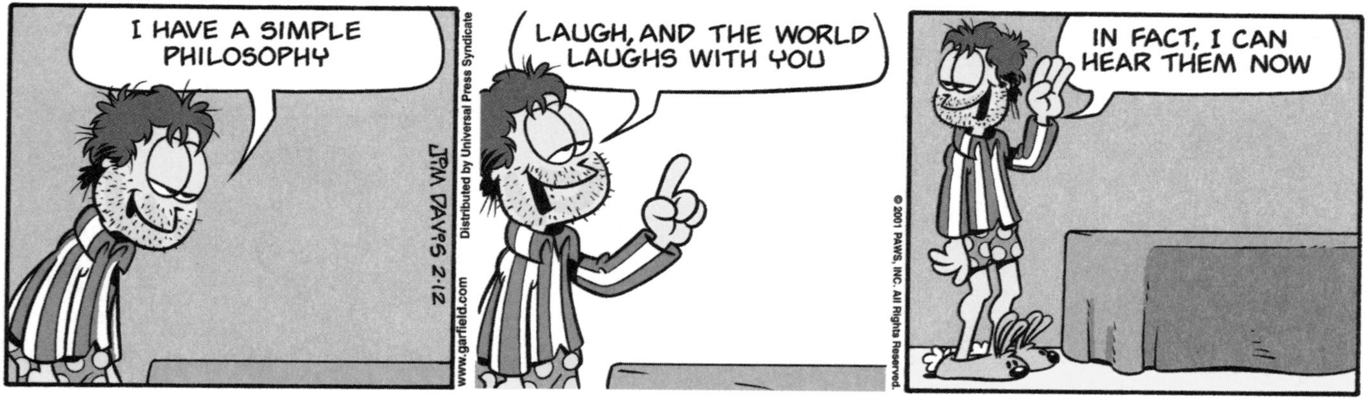
I HAVE A SIMPLE PHILOSOPHY
JIM DAVIS 2·12
Distributed by Universal Press Syndicate
www.garfield.com
LAUGH, AND THE WORLD LAUGHS WITH YOU
© 2001 PAWS, INC. All Rights Reserved.
IN FACT, I CAN HEAR THEM NOW

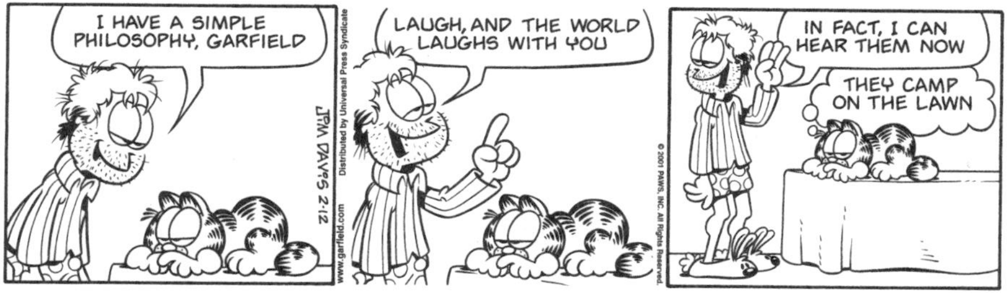
I HAVE A SIMPLE PHILOSOPHY, GARFIELD
JIM DAVIS 2·12
Distributed by Universal Press Syndicate
www.garfield.com
LAUGH, AND THE WORLD LAUGHS WITH YOU
IN FACT, I CAN HEAR THEM NOW
THEY CAMP ON THE LAWN

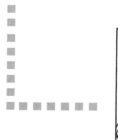

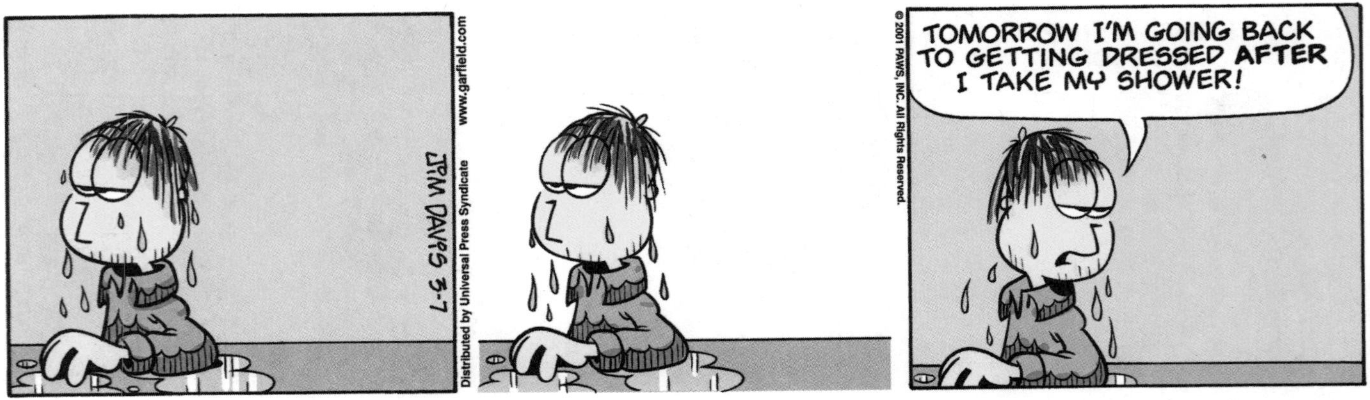
www.garfield.com
JIM DAVIS 3-7
Distributed by Universal Press Syndicate
© 2001 PAWS, INC. All Rights Reserved.
TOMORROW I'M GOING BACK TO GETTING DRESSED AFTER I TAKE MY SHOWER!

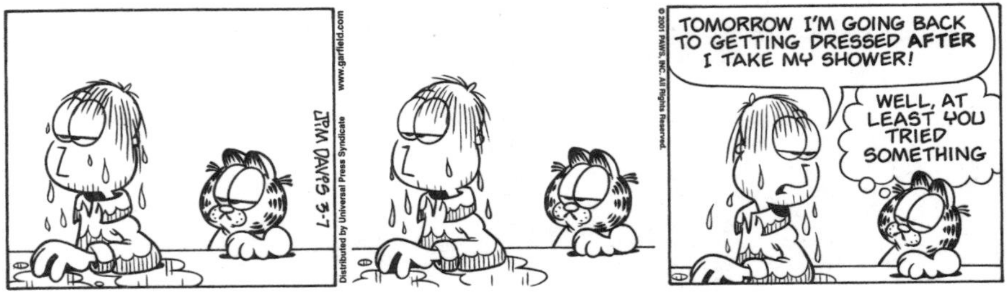
www.garfield.com
JIM DAVIS 3-7
Distributed by Universal Press Syndicate
© 2001 PAWS, INC. All Rights Reserved.
TOMORROW I'M GOING BACK TO GETTING DRESSED AFTER I TAKE MY SHOWER!
WELL, AT LEAST YOU TRIED SOMETHING

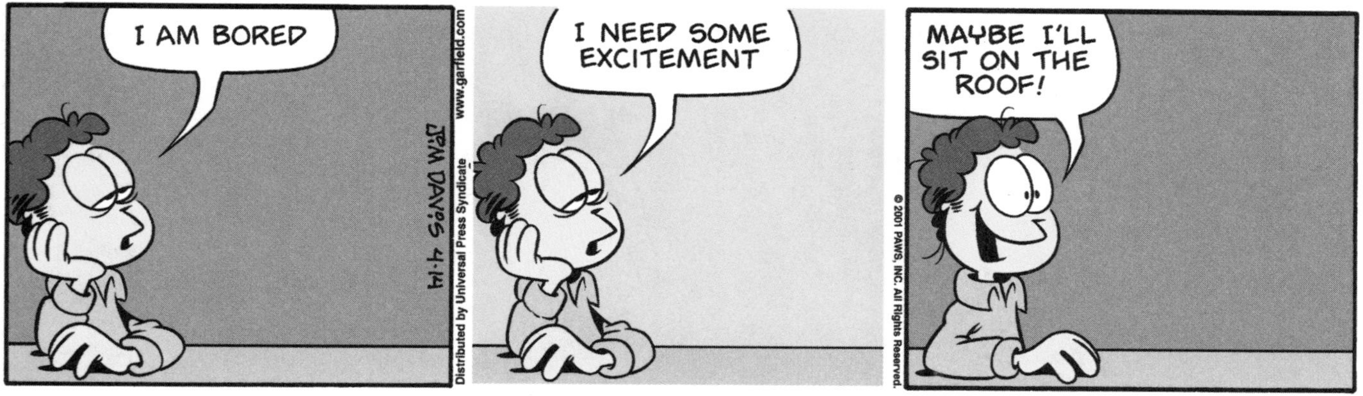
I AM BORED
I NEED SOME EXCITEMENT
MAYBE I'LL SIT ON THE ROOF!
JIM DAVIS 4-14
www.garfield.com
Distributed by Universal Press Syndicate
© 2001 PAWS, INC. All Rights Reserved.

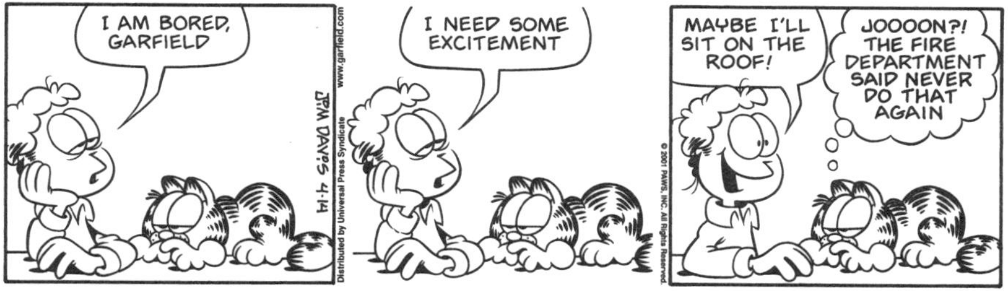
I AM BORED, GARFIELD
I NEED SOME EXCITEMENT
MAYBE I'LL SIT ON THE ROOF!
JOOOON?! THE FIRE DEPARTMENT SAID NEVER DO THAT AGAIN

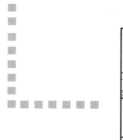

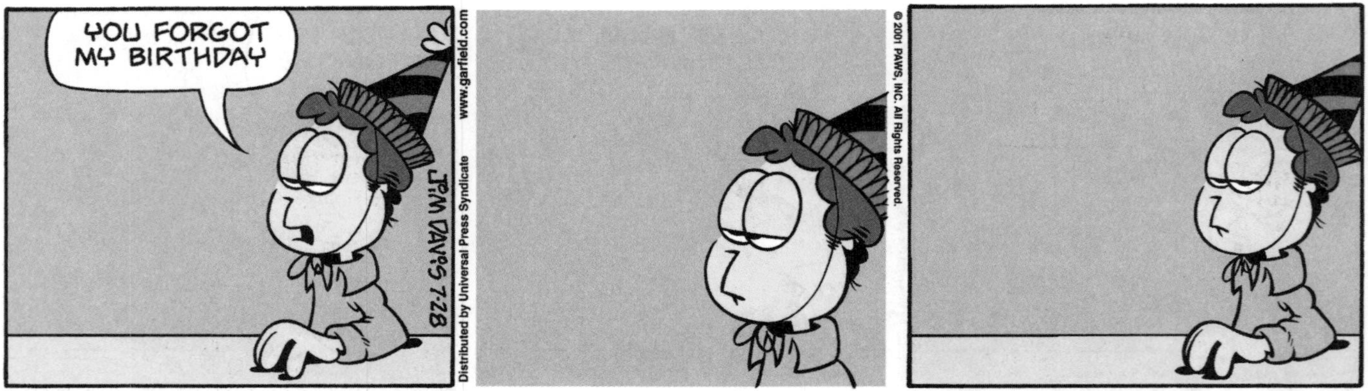
YOU FORGOT MY BIRTHDAY
JIM DAVIS 7-28
Distributed by Universal Press Syndicate www.garfield.com
© 2001 PAWS, INC. All Rights Reserved.

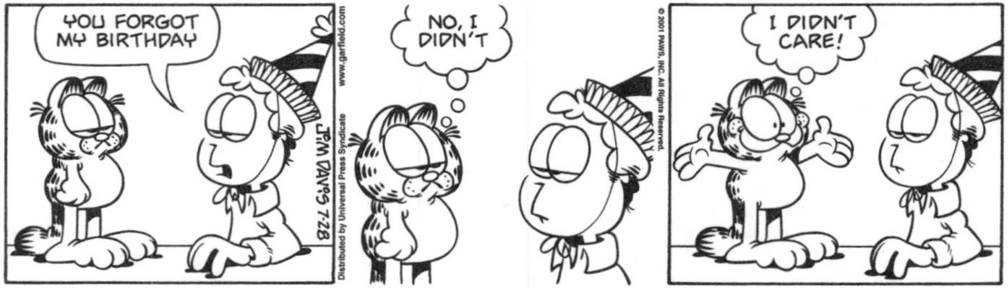
YOU FORGOT MY BIRTHDAY
JIM DAVIS 7-28
Distributed by Universal Press Syndicate www.garfield.com
NO, I DIDN'T
© 2001 PAWS, INC. All Rights Reserved.
I DIDN'T CARE!

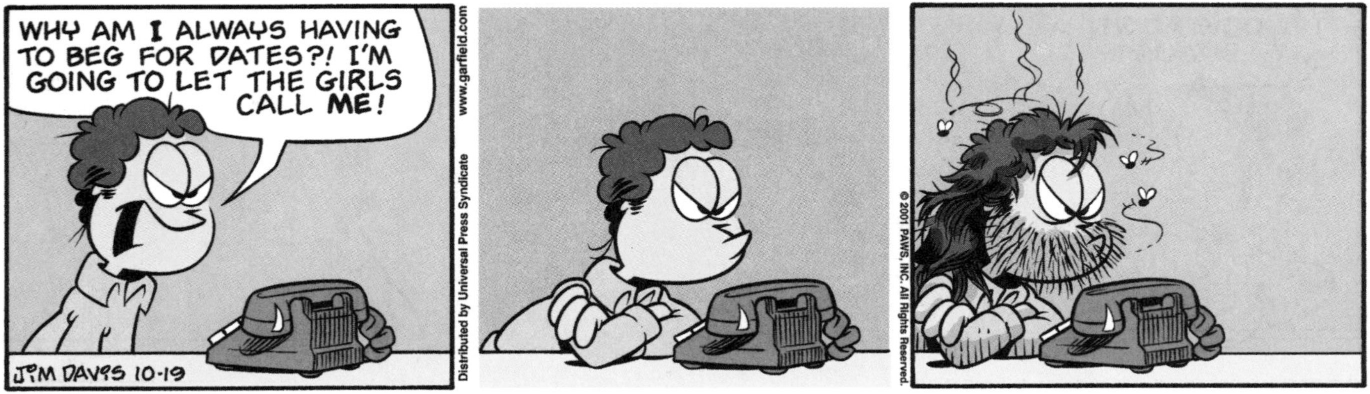
WHY AM I ALWAYS HAVING TO BEG FOR DATES?! I'M GOING TO LET THE GIRLS CALL ME!
JIM DAVIS 10-19
www.garfield.com
Distributed by Universal Press Syndicate
© 2001 PAWS, INC. All Rights Reserved.

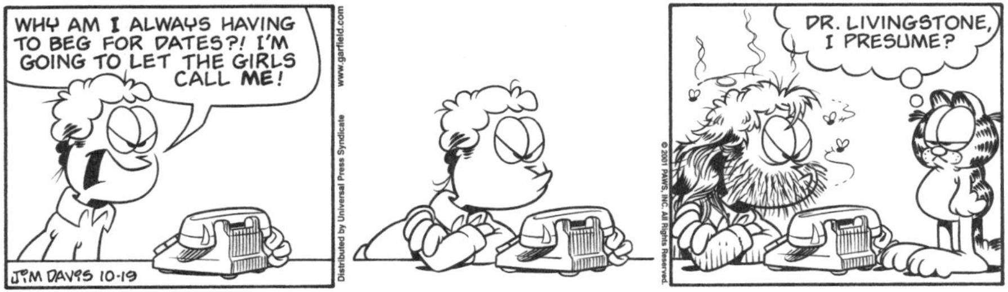
WHY AM I ALWAYS HAVING TO BEG FOR DATES?! I'M GOING TO LET THE GIRLS CALL ME!
JIM DAVIS 10-19
www.garfield.com
Distributed by Universal Press Syndicate
DR. LIVINGSTONE, I PRESUME?
© 2001 PAWS, INC. All Rights Reserved.

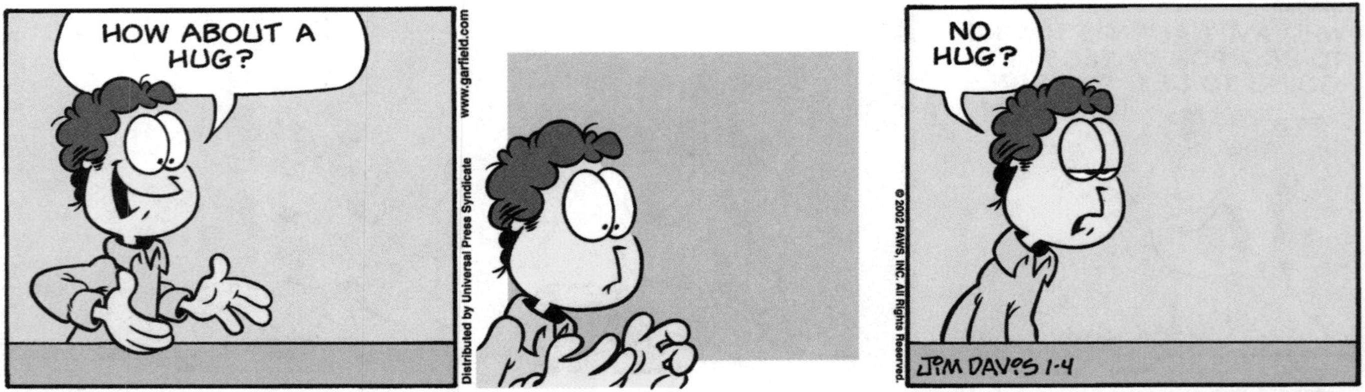
HOW ABOUT A HUG?
www.garfield.com
Distributed by Universal Press Syndicate
© 2002 PAWS, INC. All Rights Reserved.
NO HUG?
JIM DAVIS 1-4

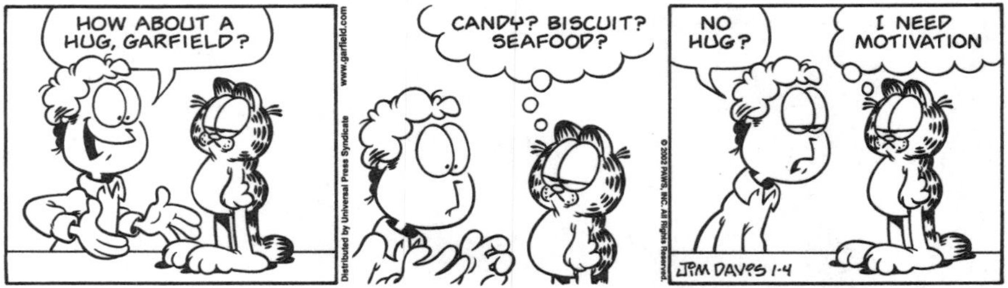
HOW ABOUT A HUG, GARFIELD?
www.garfield.com
Distributed by Universal Press Syndicate
CANDY? BISCUIT? SEAFOOD?
© 2002 PAWS, INC. All Rights Reserved.
NO HUG?
I NEED MOTIVATION
JIM DAVIS 1-4

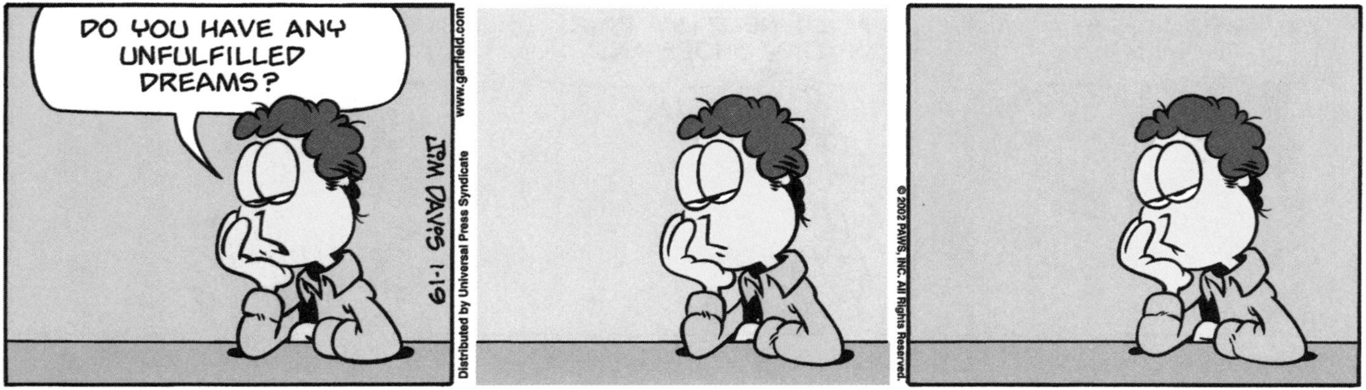
DO YOU HAVE ANY UNFULFILLED DREAMS?
JIM DAVIS 1-19
Distributed by Universal Press Syndicate
www.garfield.com
© 2002 PAWS, INC. All Rights Reserved.

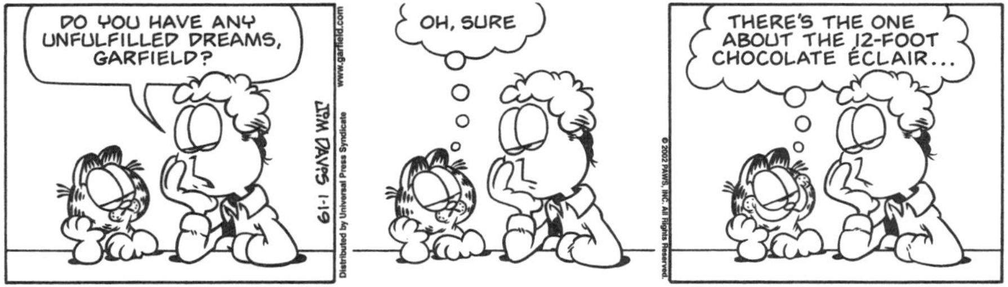
DO YOU HAVE ANY UNFULFILLED DREAMS, GARFIELD?
JIM DAVIS 1-19
Distributed by Universal Press Syndicate
www.garfield.com
OH, SURE
© 2002 PAWS, INC. All Rights Reserved.
THERE'S THE ONE ABOUT THE 12-FOOT CHOCOLATE ÉCLAIR...

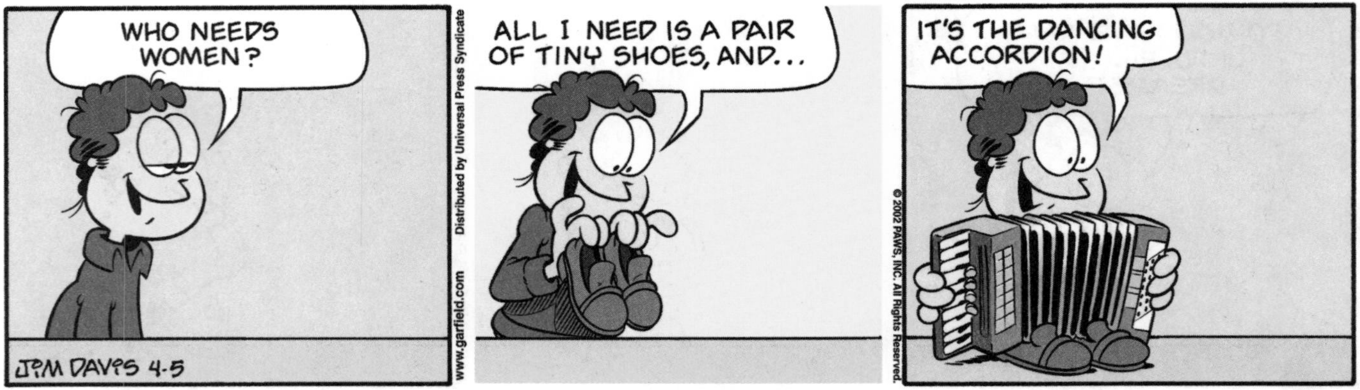
WHO NEEDS WOMEN?
ALL I NEED IS A PAIR OF TINY SHOES, AND...
IT'S THE DANCING ACCORDION!
JIM DAVIS 4-5
www.garfield.com Distributed by Universal Press Syndicate
© 2002 PAWS, INC. All Rights Reserved.

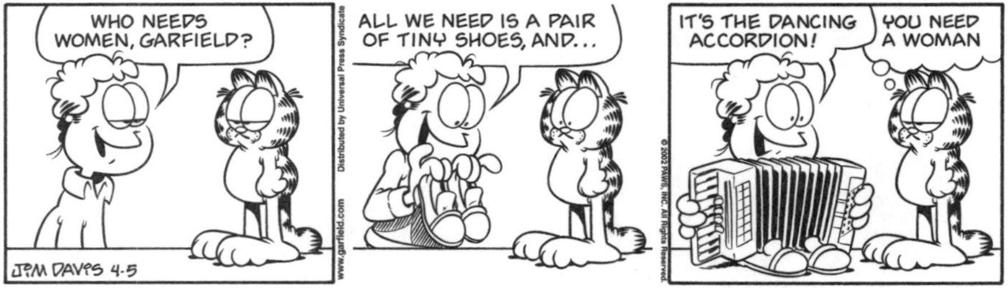
WHO NEEDS WOMEN, GARFIELD?
ALL WE NEED IS A PAIR OF TINY SHOES, AND...
IT'S THE DANCING ACCORDION!
YOU NEED A WOMAN
JIM DAVIS 4-5
www.garfield.com Distributed by Universal Press Syndicate
© 2002 PAWS, INC. All Rights Reserved.

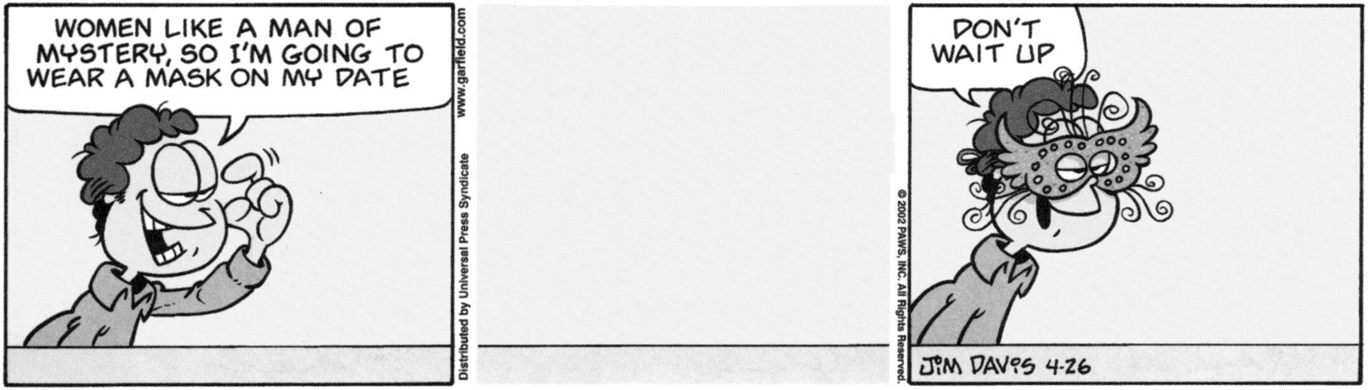
WOMEN LIKE A MAN OF MYSTERY, SO I'M GOING TO WEAR A MASK ON MY DATE
www.garfield.com
Distributed by Universal Press Syndicate
© 2002 PAWS, INC. All Rights Reserved.
DON'T WAIT UP
JIM DAVIS 4-26

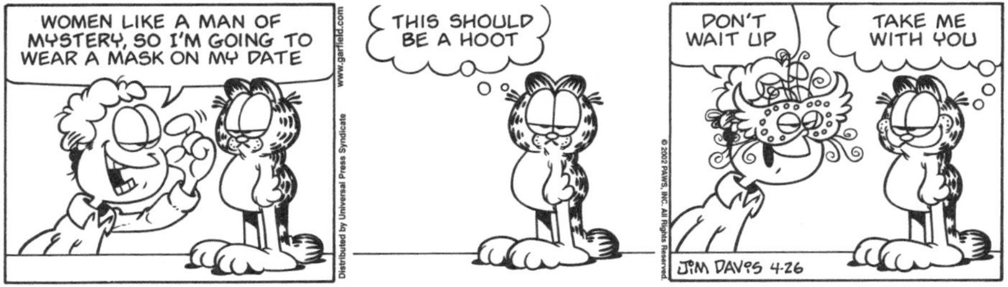
WOMEN LIKE A MAN OF MYSTERY, SO I'M GOING TO WEAR A MASK ON MY DATE
www.garfield.com
Distributed by Universal Press Syndicate
THIS SHOULD BE A HOOT
© 2002 PAWS, INC. All Rights Reserved.
DON'T WAIT UP
TAKE ME WITH YOU
JIM DAVIS 4-26

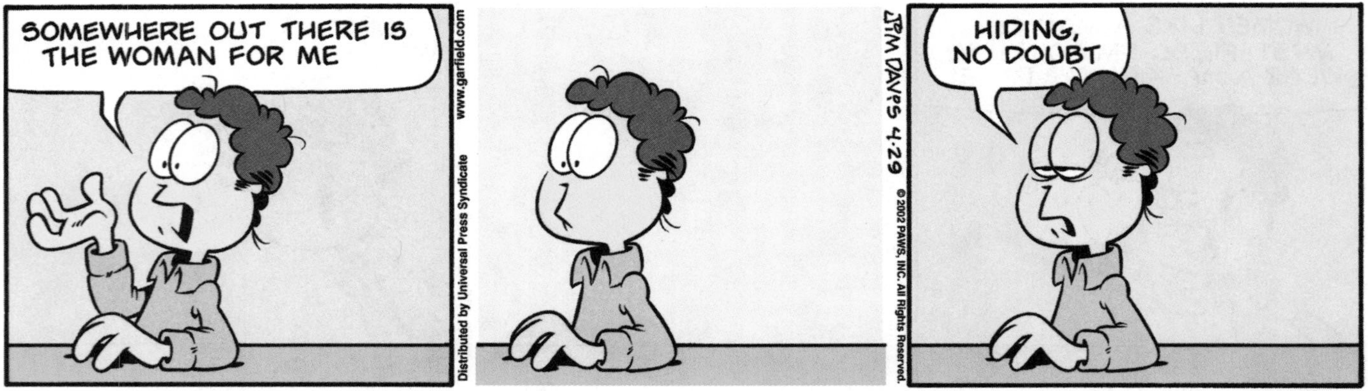
SOMEWHERE OUT THERE IS THE WOMAN FOR ME
www.garfield.com
Distributed by Universal Press Syndicate
JIM DAVIS 4-29
© 2002 PAWS, INC. All Rights Reserved.
HIDING, NO DOUBT

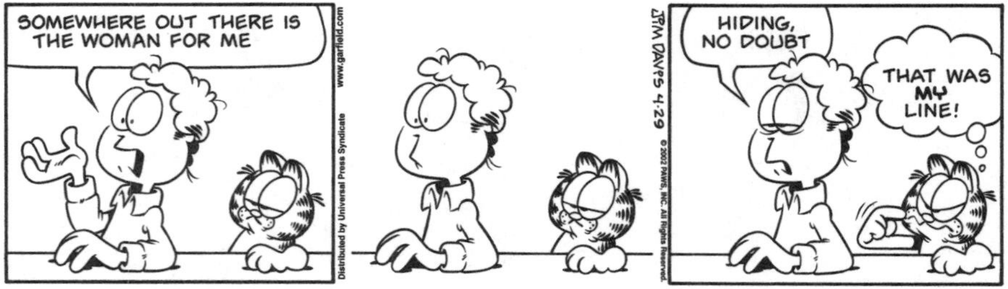
SOMEWHERE OUT THERE IS THE WOMAN FOR ME
www.garfield.com
Distributed by Universal Press Syndicate
JIM DAVIS 4-29
HIDING, NO DOUBT
THAT WAS MY LINE!

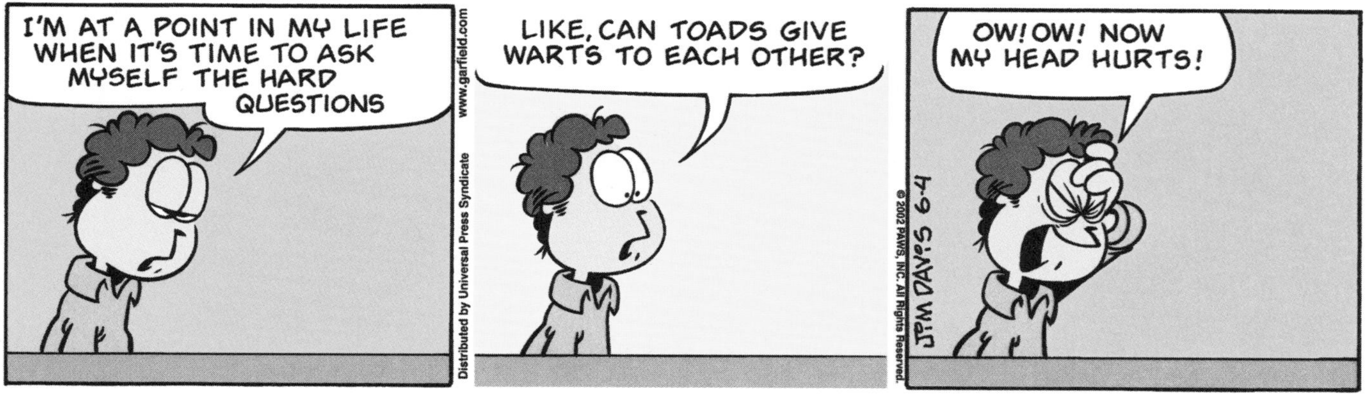
I'M AT A POINT IN MY LIFE WHEN IT'S TIME TO ASK MYSELF THE HARD QUESTIONS
LIKE, CAN TOADS GIVE WARTS TO EACH OTHER?
OW! OW! NOW MY HEAD HURTS!
www.garfield.com
Distributed by Universal Press Syndicate
© 2002 PAWS, INC. All Rights Reserved.
JIM DAVIS 6-4

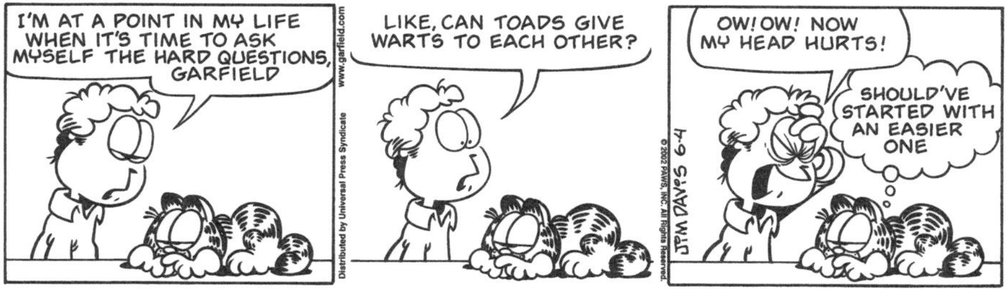
I'M AT A POINT IN MY LIFE WHEN IT'S TIME TO ASK MYSELF THE HARD QUESTIONS, GARFIELD
LIKE, CAN TOADS GIVE WARTS TO EACH OTHER?
OW! OW! NOW MY HEAD HURTS!
SHOULD'VE STARTED WITH AN EASIER ONE

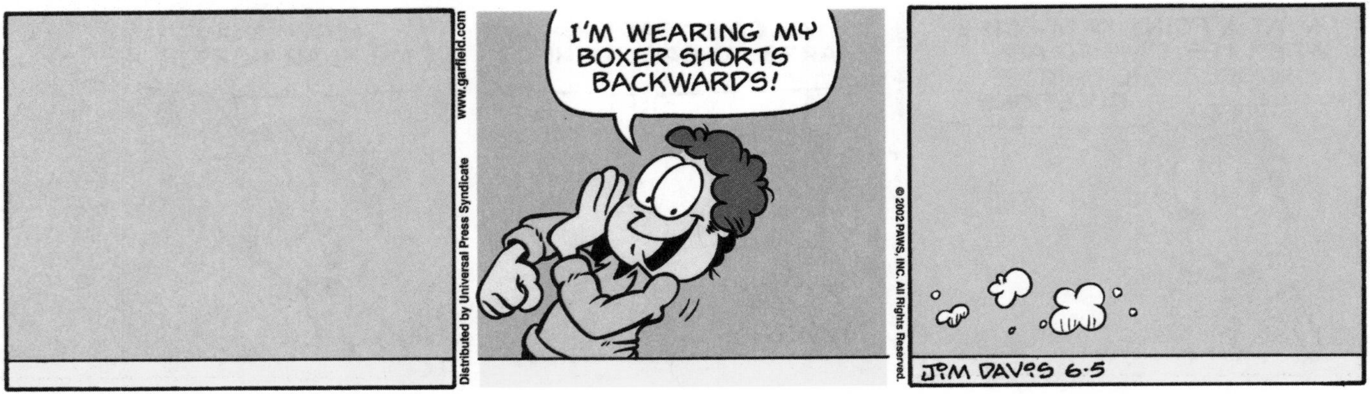
www.garfield.com
Distributed by Universal Press Syndicate
I'M WEARING MY BOXER SHORTS BACKWARDS!
© 2002 PAWS, INC. All Rights Reserved.
JIM DAVIS 6-5

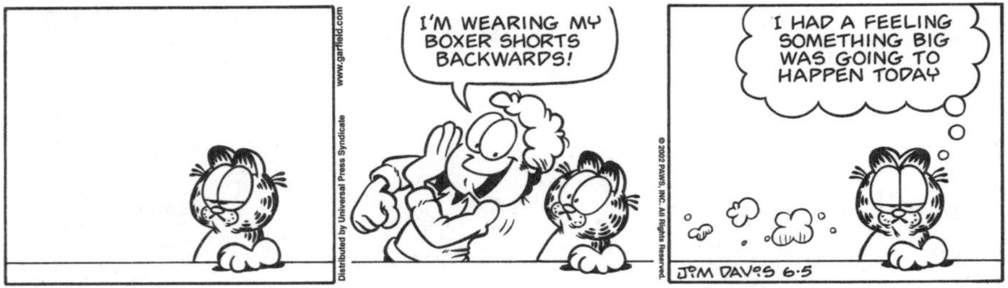
www.garfield.com
Distributed by Universal Press Syndicate
I'M WEARING MY BOXER SHORTS BACKWARDS!
© 2002 PAWS, INC. All Rights Reserved.
I HAD A FEELING SOMETHING BIG WAS GOING TO HAPPEN TODAY
JIM DAVIS 6-5

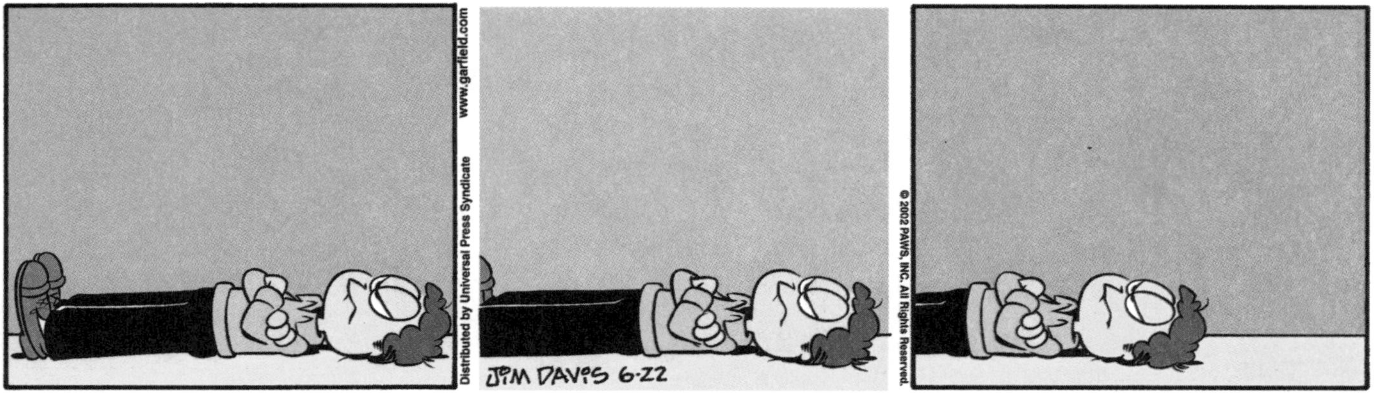
www.garfield.com
Distributed by Universal Press Syndicate
JIM DAVIS 6-22
© 2002 PAWS, INC. All Rights Reserved.

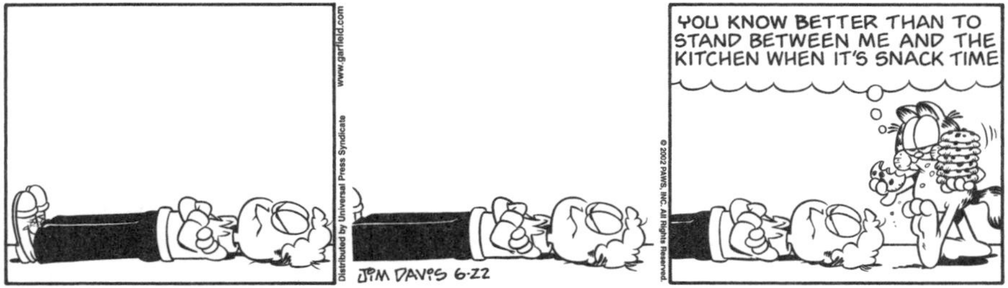
www.garfield.com
Distributed by Universal Press Syndicate
JIM DAVIS 6-22
© 2002 PAWS, INC. All Rights Reserved.
YOU KNOW BETTER THAN TO STAND BETWEEN ME AND THE KITCHEN WHEN IT'S SNACK TIME

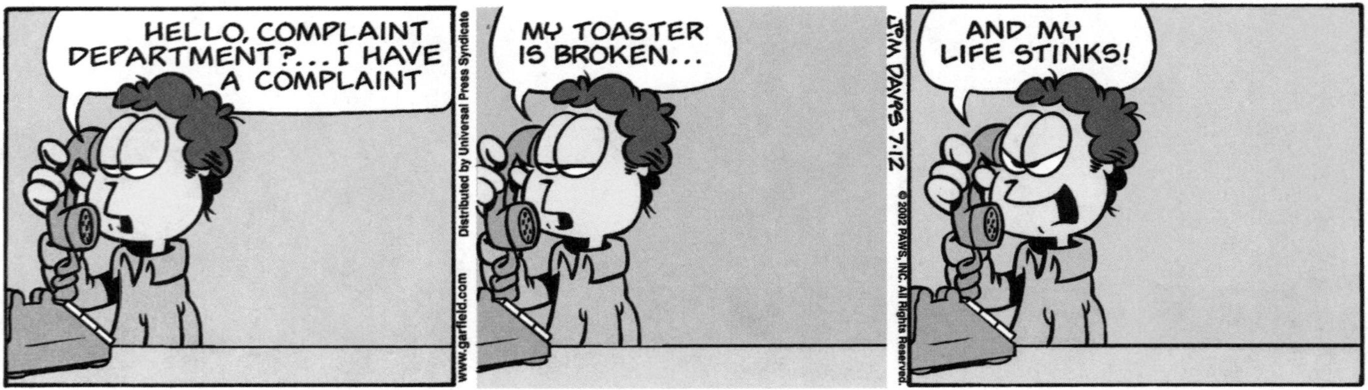
HELLO, COMPLAINT DEPARTMENT?... I HAVE A COMPLAINT
MY TOASTER IS BROKEN...
AND MY LIFE STINKS!
Distributed by Universal Press Syndicate
www.garfield.com
JPM DAVIS 7·12
© 2002 PAWS, INC. All Rights Reserved.

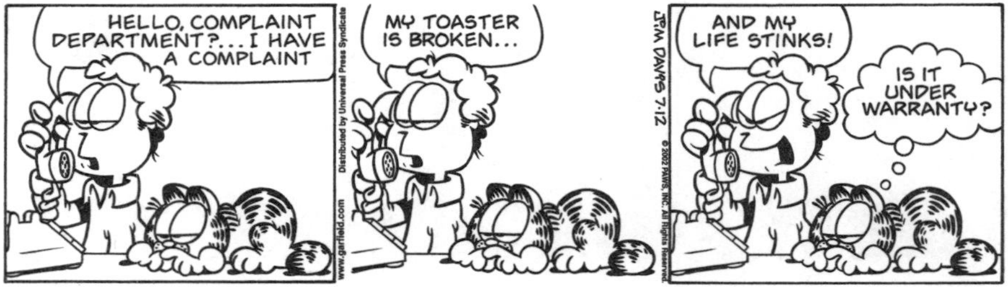
HELLO, COMPLAINT DEPARTMENT?... I HAVE A COMPLAINT
MY TOASTER IS BROKEN...
AND MY LIFE STINKS!
IS IT UNDER WARRANTY?
Distributed by Universal Press Syndicate
www.garfield.com
JPM DAVIS 7·12
© 2002 PAWS, INC. All Rights Reserved.

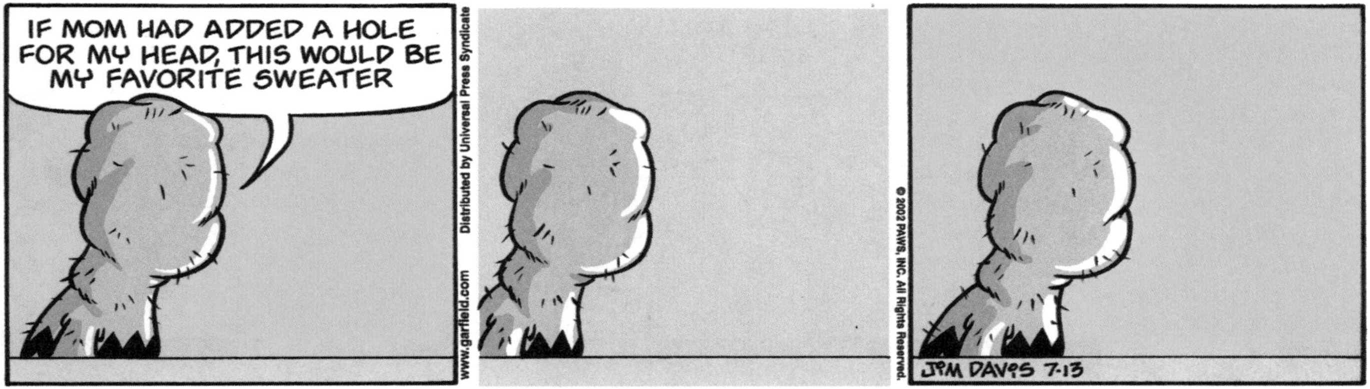
IF MOM HAD ADDED A HOLE FOR MY HEAD, THIS WOULD BE MY FAVORITE SWEATER
www.garfield.com Distributed by Universal Press Syndicate
© 2002 PAWS, INC. All Rights Reserved.
JIM DAVIS 7-13

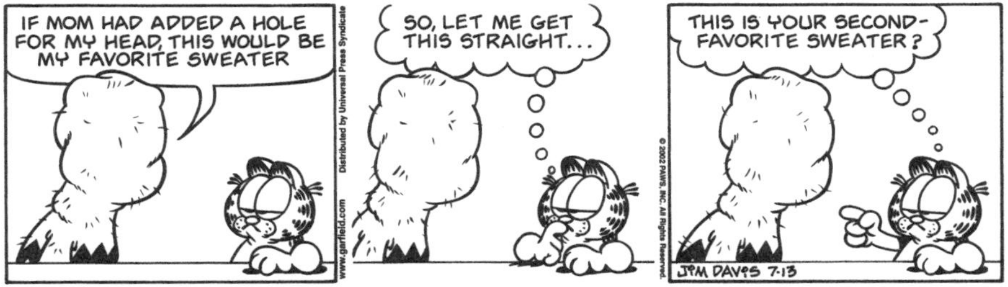
IF MOM HAD ADDED A HOLE FOR MY HEAD, THIS WOULD BE MY FAVORITE SWEATER
SO, LET ME GET THIS STRAIGHT...
THIS IS YOUR SECOND-FAVORITE SWEATER?
JIM DAVIS 7-13

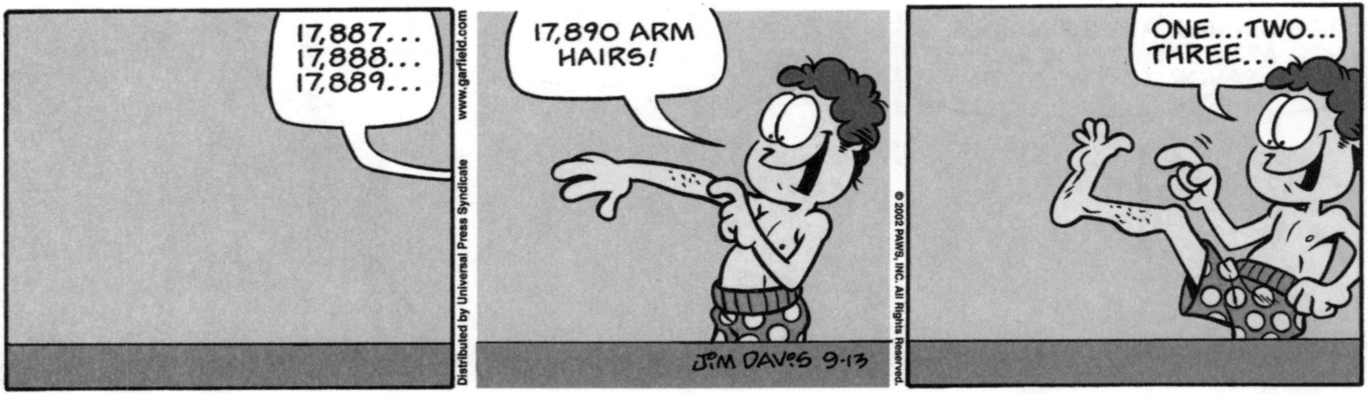
17,887...
17,888...
17,889...
Distributed by Universal Press Syndicate www.garfield.com
17,890 ARM HAIRS!
JIM DAVIS 9-13
© 2002 PAWS, INC. All Rights Reserved.
ONE...TWO... THREE...

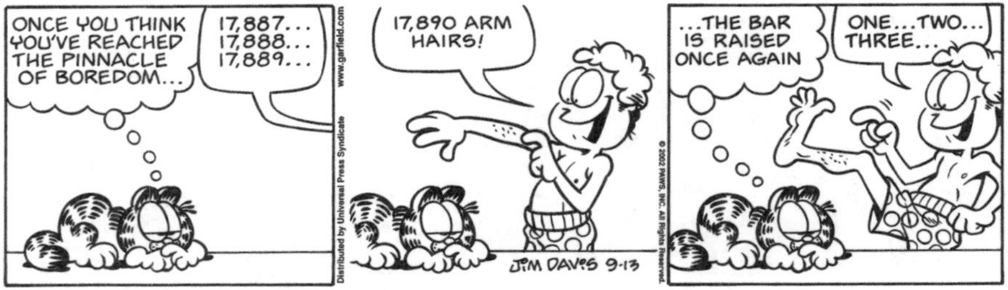
ONCE YOU THINK YOU'VE REACHED THE PINNACLE OF BOREDOM...
17,887...
17,888...
17,889...
Distributed by Universal Press Syndicate www.garfield.com
17,890 ARM HAIRS!
JIM DAVIS 9-13
© 2002 PAWS, INC. All Rights Reserved.
...THE BAR IS RAISED ONCE AGAIN
ONE...TWO... THREE...

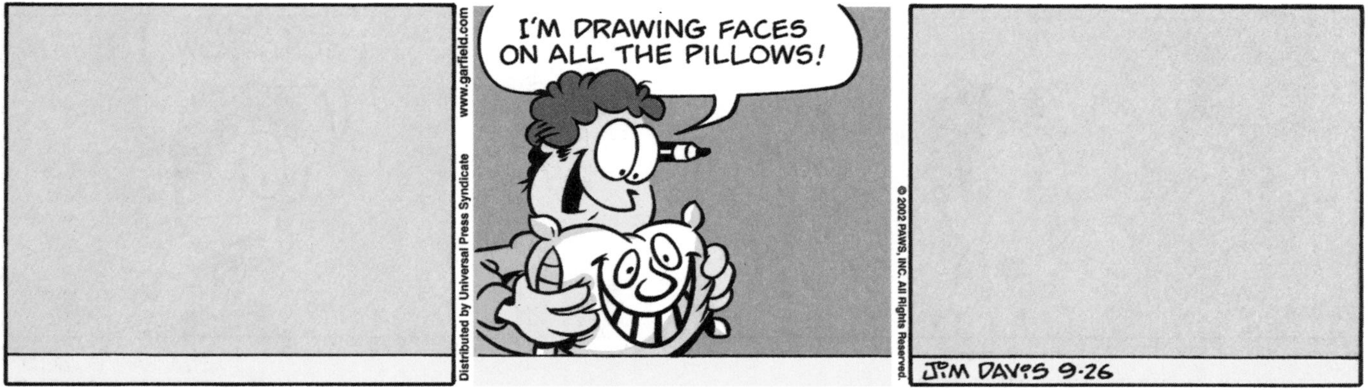
Distributed by Universal Press Syndicate www.garfield.com
I'M DRAWING FACES ON ALL THE PILLOWS!
© 2002 PAWS, INC. All Rights Reserved.
JIM DAVIS 9-26

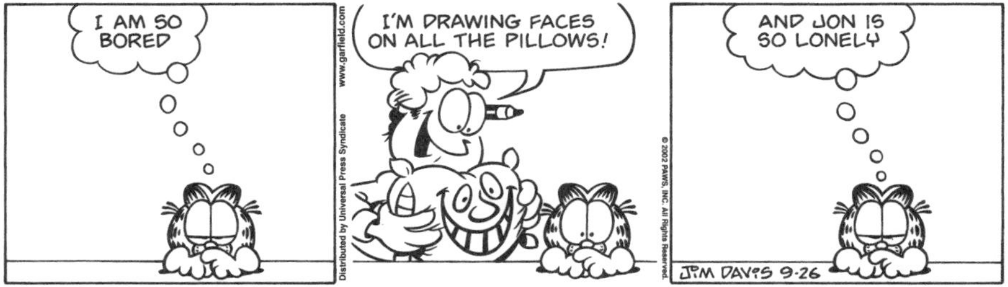
I AM SO BORED
Distributed by Universal Press Syndicate www.garfield.com
I'M DRAWING FACES ON ALL THE PILLOWS!
© 2002 PAWS, INC. All Rights Reserved.
AND JON IS SO LONELY
JIM DAVIS 9-26

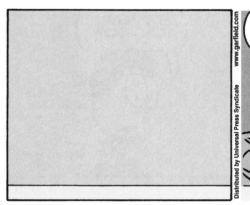

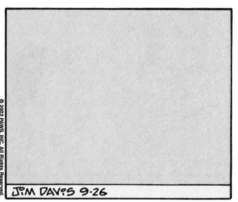

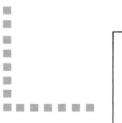

56

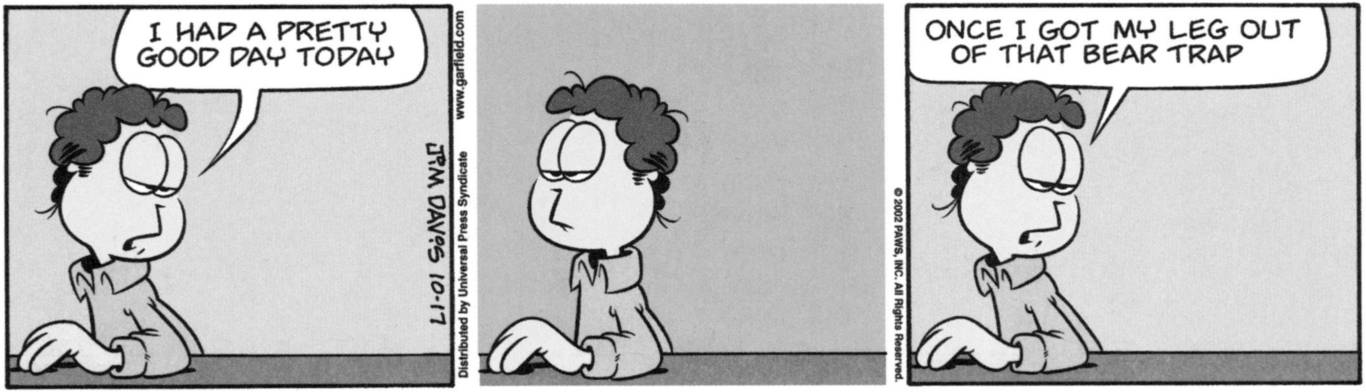
I HAD A PRETTY GOOD DAY TODAY
JPM DAVIS 10-17
www.garfield.com
Distributed by Universal Press Syndicate
© 2002 PAWS, INC. All Rights Reserved.
ONCE I GOT MY LEG OUT OF THAT BEAR TRAP

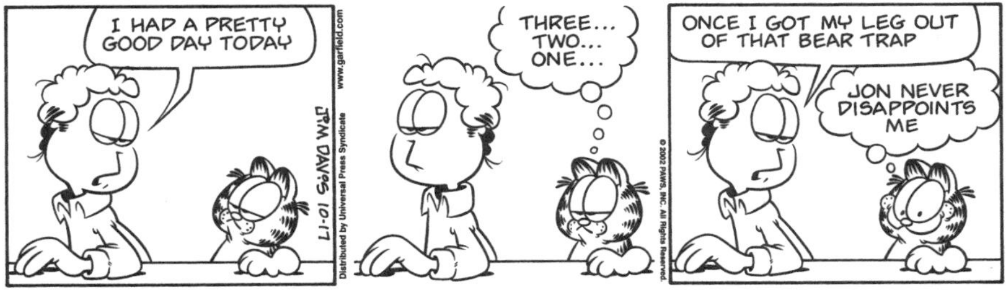
I HAD A PRETTY GOOD DAY TODAY
JPM DAVIS 10-17
www.garfield.com
Distributed by Universal Press Syndicate
THREE... TWO... ONE...
© 2002 PAWS, INC. All Rights Reserved.
ONCE I GOT MY LEG OUT OF THAT BEAR TRAP
JON NEVER DISAPPOINTS ME

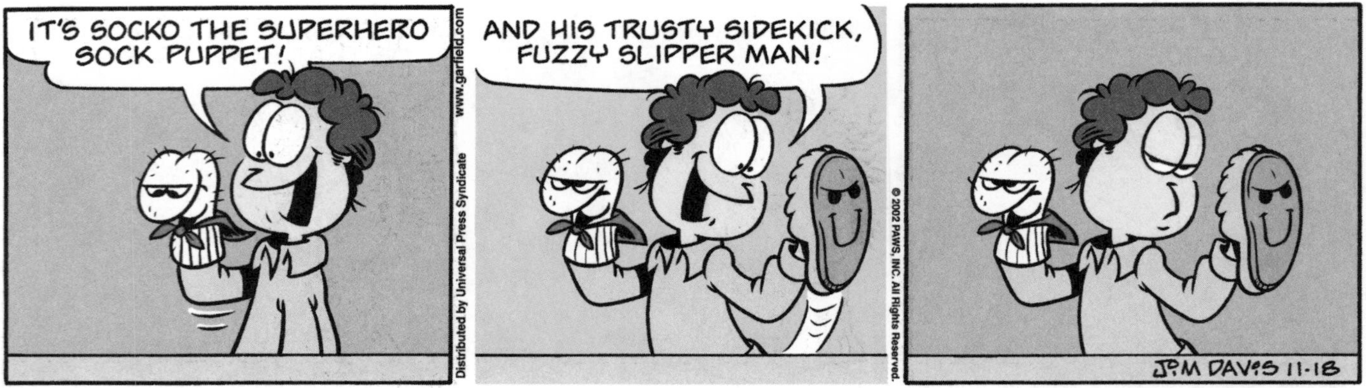
IT'S SOCKO THE SUPERHERO SOCK PUPPET!
www.garfield.com
Distributed by Universal Press Syndicate
AND HIS TRUSTY SIDEKICK, FUZZY SLIPPER MAN!
© 2002 PAWS, INC. All Rights Reserved.
JIM DAVIS 11-18

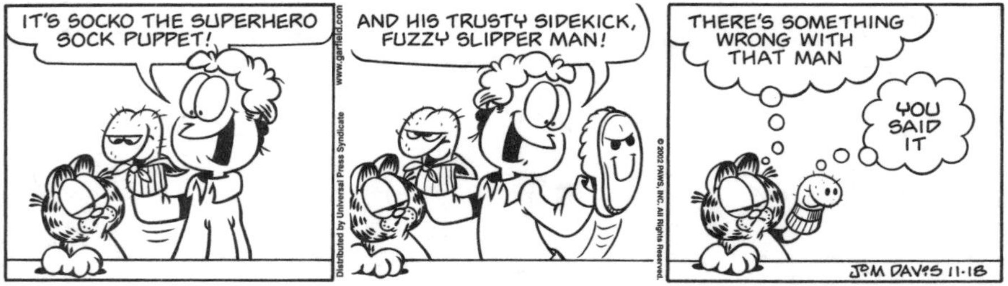
IT'S SOCKO THE SUPERHERO SOCK PUPPET!
www.garfield.com
Distributed by Universal Press Syndicate
AND HIS TRUSTY SIDEKICK, FUZZY SLIPPER MAN!
© 2002 PAWS, INC. All Rights Reserved.
THERE'S SOMETHING WRONG WITH THAT MAN
YOU SAID IT
JIM DAVIS 11-18

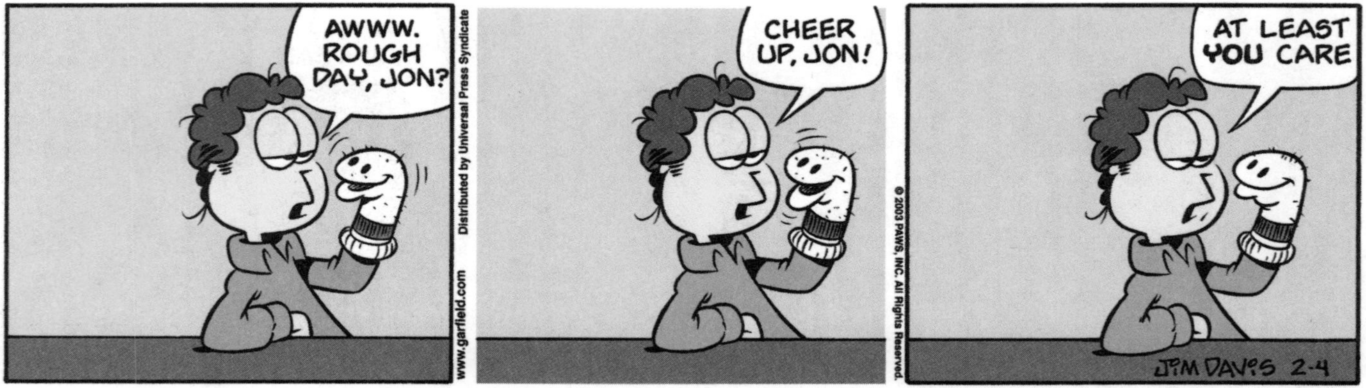
AWWW. ROUGH DAY, JON?
CHEER UP, JON!
AT LEAST YOU CARE
JIM DAVIS 2-4
www.garfield.com Distributed by Universal Press Syndicate
© 2003 PAWS, INC. All Rights Reserved.

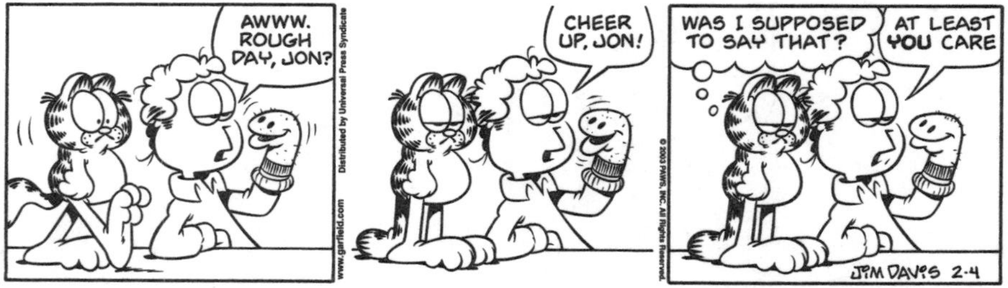
AWWW. ROUGH DAY, JON?
CHEER UP, JON!
WAS I SUPPOSED TO SAY THAT?
AT LEAST YOU CARE
JIM DAVIS 2-4
www.garfield.com Distributed by Universal Press Syndicate
© 2003 PAWS, INC. All Rights Reserved.

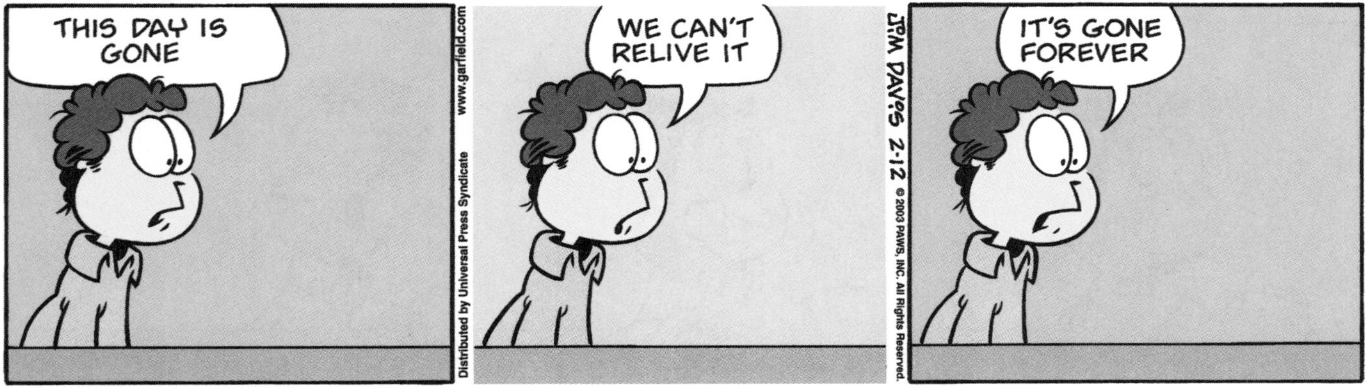
THIS DAY IS GONE
WE CAN'T RELIVE IT
IT'S GONE FOREVER
www.garfield.com
Distributed by Universal Press Syndicate
JIM DAVIS 2-12
© 2003 PAWS, INC. All Rights Reserved.

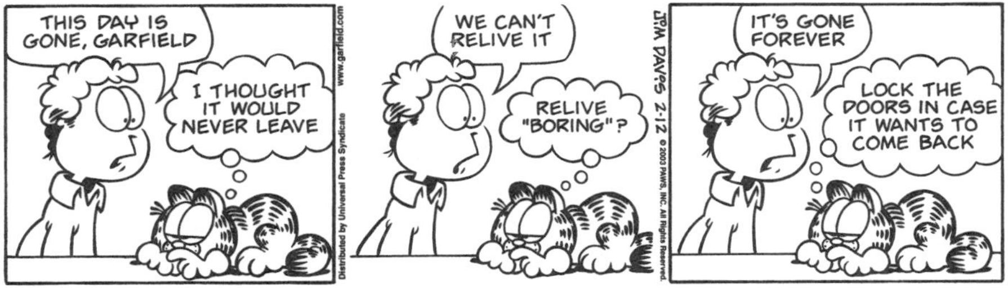
THIS DAY IS GONE, GARFIELD
I THOUGHT IT WOULD NEVER LEAVE
WE CAN'T RELIVE IT
RELIVE "BORING"?
IT'S GONE FOREVER
LOCK THE DOORS IN CASE IT WANTS TO COME BACK
www.garfield.com
Distributed by Universal Press Syndicate
JIM DAVIS 2-12
© 2003 PAWS, INC. All Rights Reserved.

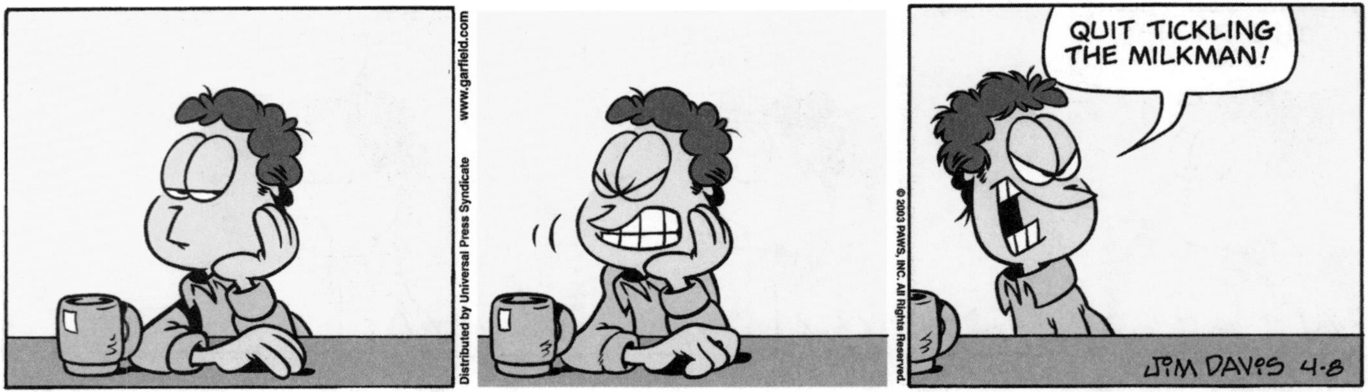
www.garfield.com
Distributed by Universal Press Syndicate
© 2003 PAWS, INC. All Rights Reserved.
QUIT TICKLING THE MILKMAN!
JIM DAVIS 4-8

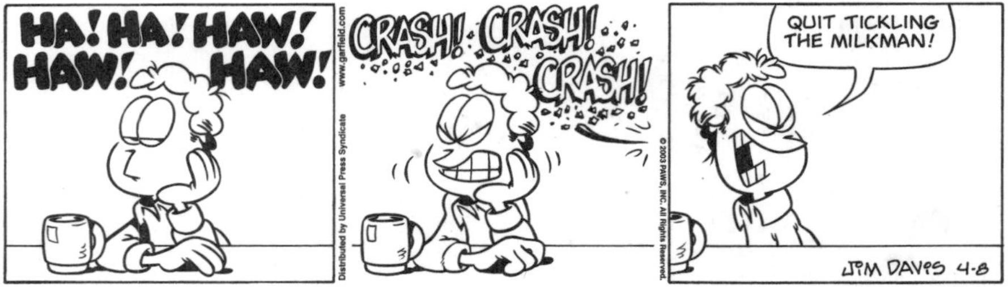
HA! HA! HAW! HAW! HAW!
www.garfield.com
Distributed by Universal Press Syndicate
CRASH! CRASH! CRASH!
© 2003 PAWS, INC. All Rights Reserved.
QUIT TICKLING THE MILKMAN!
JIM DAVIS 4-8

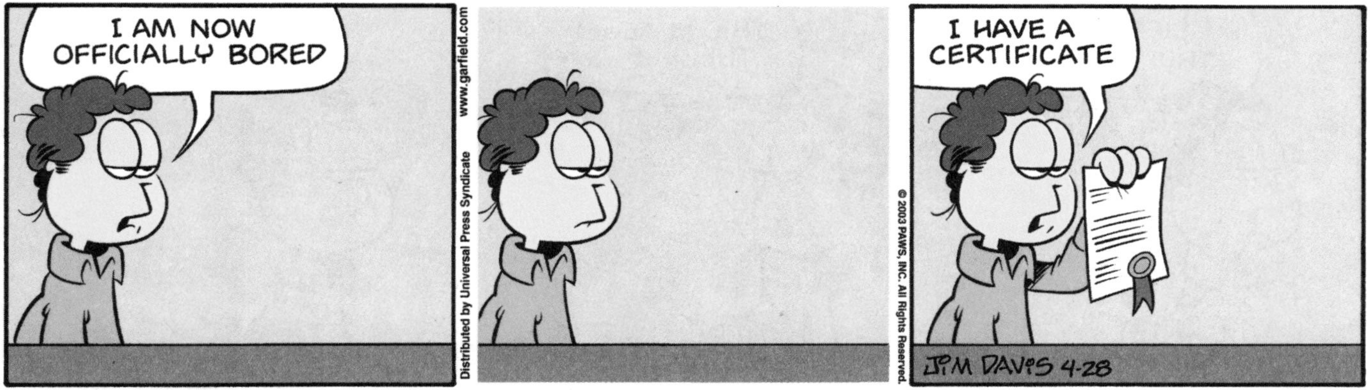
I AM NOW OFFICIALLY BORED
www.garfield.com
Distributed by Universal Press Syndicate
© 2003 PAWS, INC. All Rights Reserved.
I HAVE A CERTIFICATE
JIM DAVIS 4-28

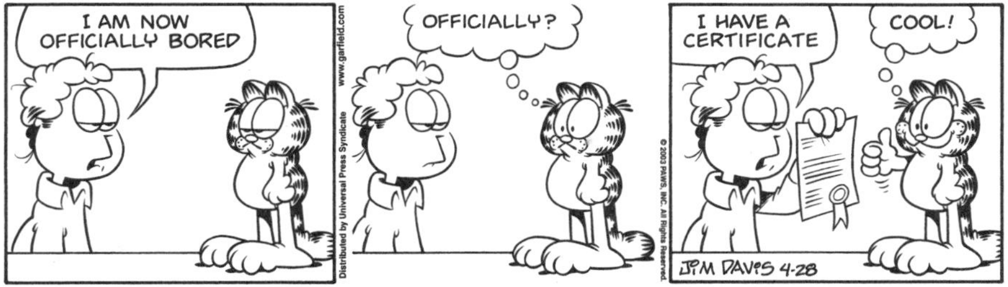
I AM NOW OFFICIALLY BORED
OFFICIALLY?
I HAVE A CERTIFICATE
COOL!
JIM DAVIS 4-28

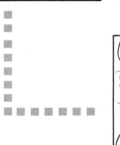

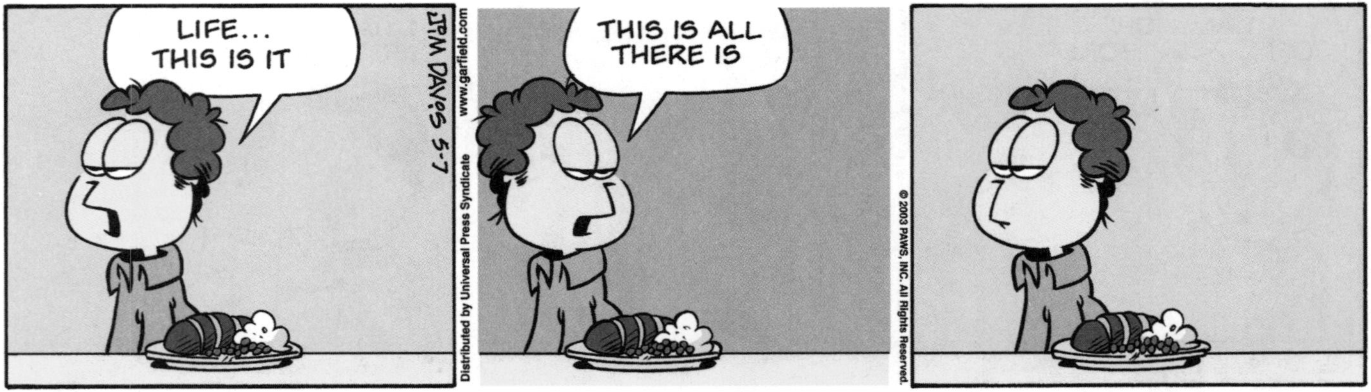
LIFE...
THIS IS IT
JPM DAVIS 5-7
www.garfield.com
Distributed by Universal Press Syndicate
THIS IS ALL
THERE IS
© 2003 PAWS, INC. All Rights Reserved.

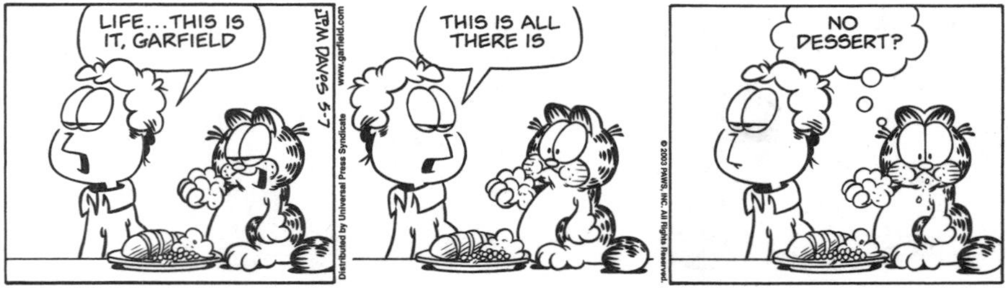
LIFE...THIS IS
IT, GARFIELD
JPM DAVIS 5-7
www.garfield.com
Distributed by Universal Press Syndicate
THIS IS ALL
THERE IS
© 2003 PAWS, INC. All Rights Reserved.
NO
DESSERT?

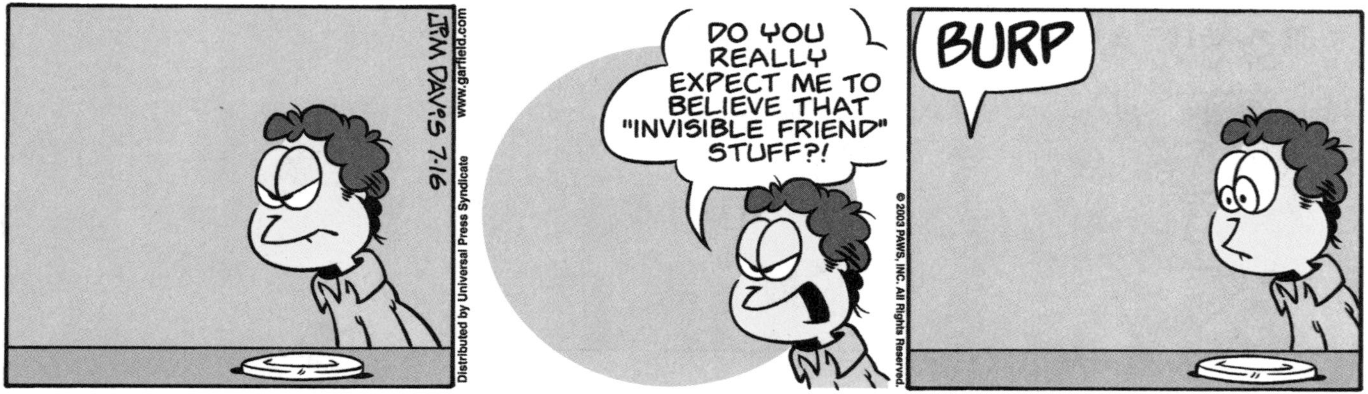
JPM DAVIS 7-16
www.garfield.com
Distributed by Universal Press Syndicate
DO YOU REALLY EXPECT ME TO BELIEVE THAT "INVISIBLE FRIEND" STUFF?!
© 2003 PAWS, INC. All Rights Reserved.
BURP

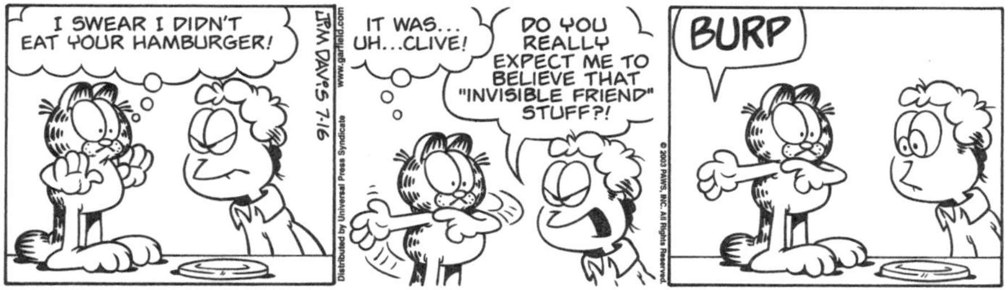
I SWEAR I DIDN'T EAT YOUR HAMBURGER!
JPM DAVIS 7-16
www.garfield.com
Distributed by Universal Press Syndicate
IT WAS... UH...CLIVE!
DO YOU REALLY EXPECT ME TO BELIEVE THAT "INVISIBLE FRIEND" STUFF?!
© 2003 PAWS, INC. All Rights Reserved.
BURP

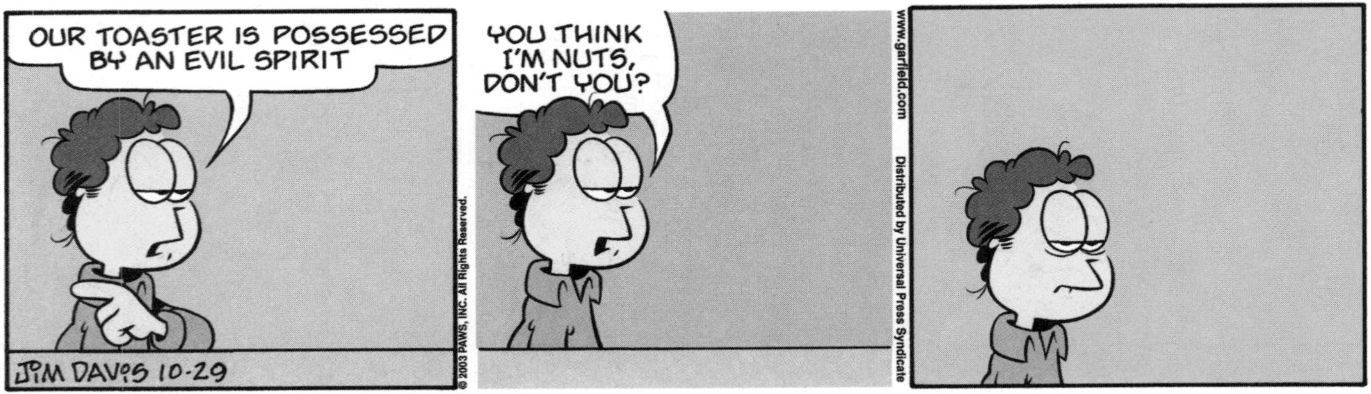
OUR TOASTER IS POSSESSED BY AN EVIL SPIRIT
JIM DAVIS 10-29
© 2003 PAWS, INC. All Rights Reserved.
YOU THINK I'M NUTS, DON'T YOU?
www.garfield.com
Distributed by Universal Press Syndicate

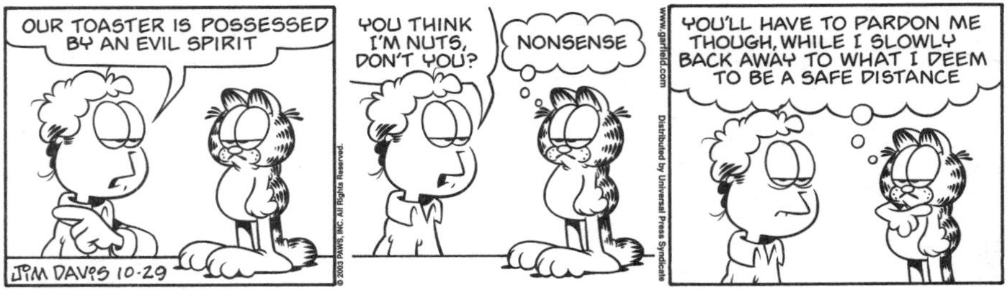
OUR TOASTER IS POSSESSED BY AN EVIL SPIRIT
JIM DAVIS 10-29
© 2003 PAWS, INC. All Rights Reserved.
YOU THINK I'M NUTS, DON'T YOU?
NONSENSE
www.garfield.com
Distributed by Universal Press Syndicate
YOU'LL HAVE TO PARDON ME THOUGH, WHILE I SLOWLY BACK AWAY TO WHAT I DEEM TO BE A SAFE DISTANCE

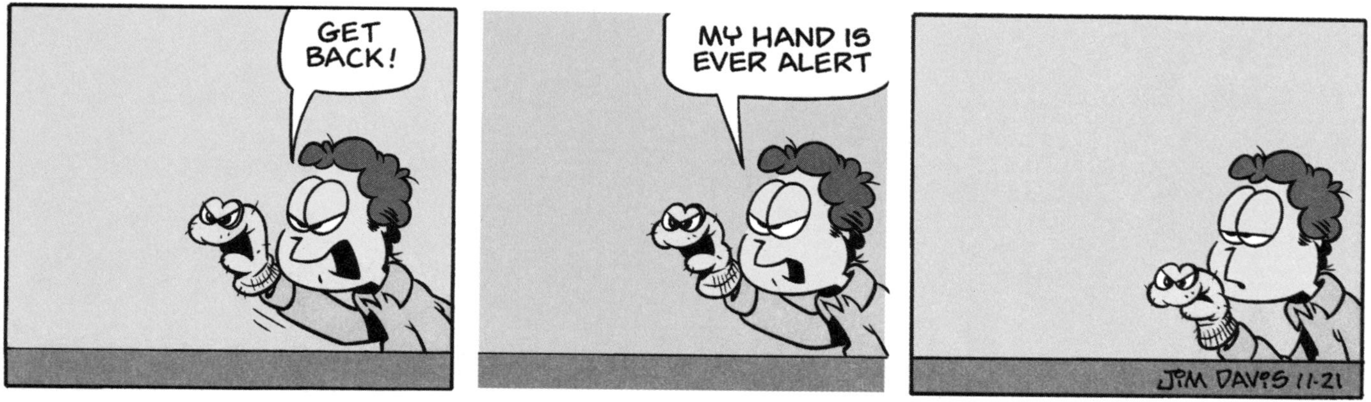
GET BACK!
MY HAND IS EVER ALERT
JIM DAVIS 11-21

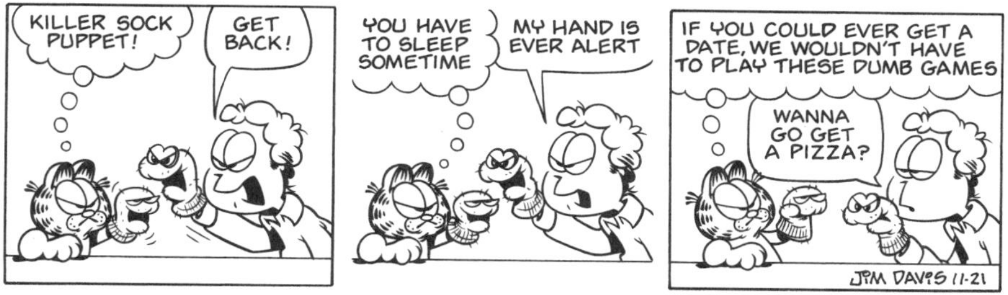
KILLER SOCK PUPPET!
GET BACK!
YOU HAVE TO SLEEP SOMETIME
MY HAND IS EVER ALERT
IF YOU COULD EVER GET A DATE, WE WOULDN'T HAVE TO PLAY THESE DUMB GAMES
WANNA GO GET A PIZZA?
JIM DAVIS 11-21

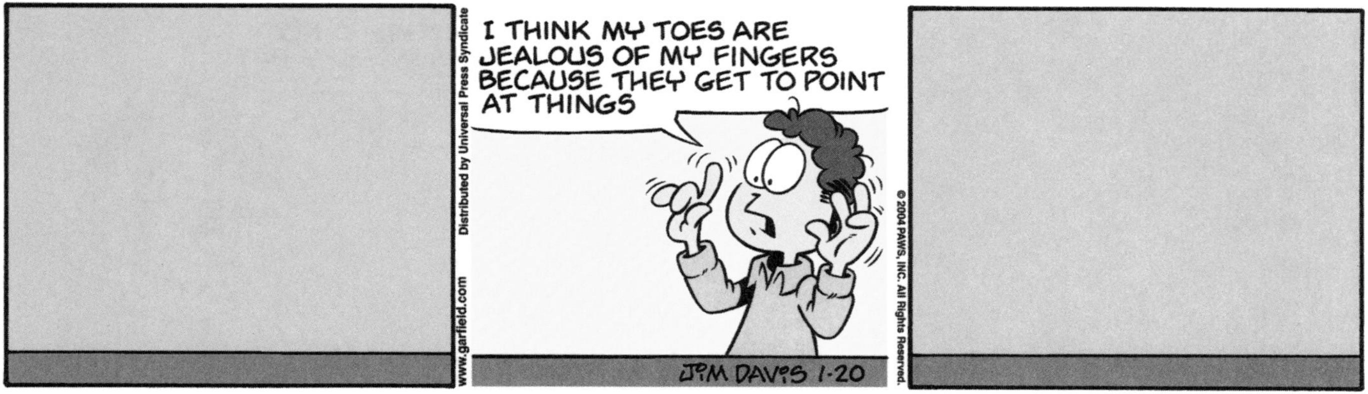
I THINK MY TOES ARE JEALOUS OF MY FINGERS BECAUSE THEY GET TO POINT AT THINGS
JIM DAVIS 1-20
www.garfield.com Distributed by Universal Press Syndicate
© 2004 PAWS, INC. All Rights Reserved.

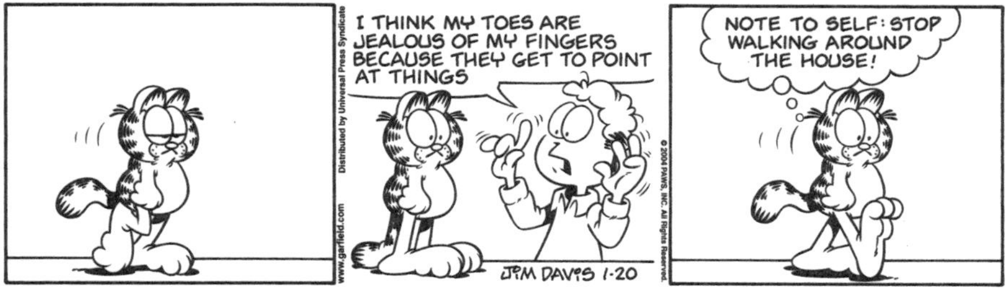
I THINK MY TOES ARE JEALOUS OF MY FINGERS BECAUSE THEY GET TO POINT AT THINGS
NOTE TO SELF: STOP WALKING AROUND THE HOUSE!
JIM DAVIS 1-20

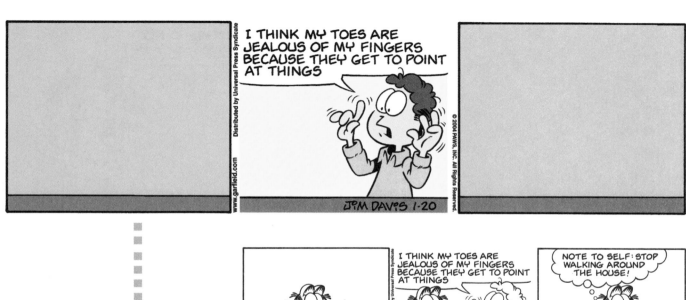

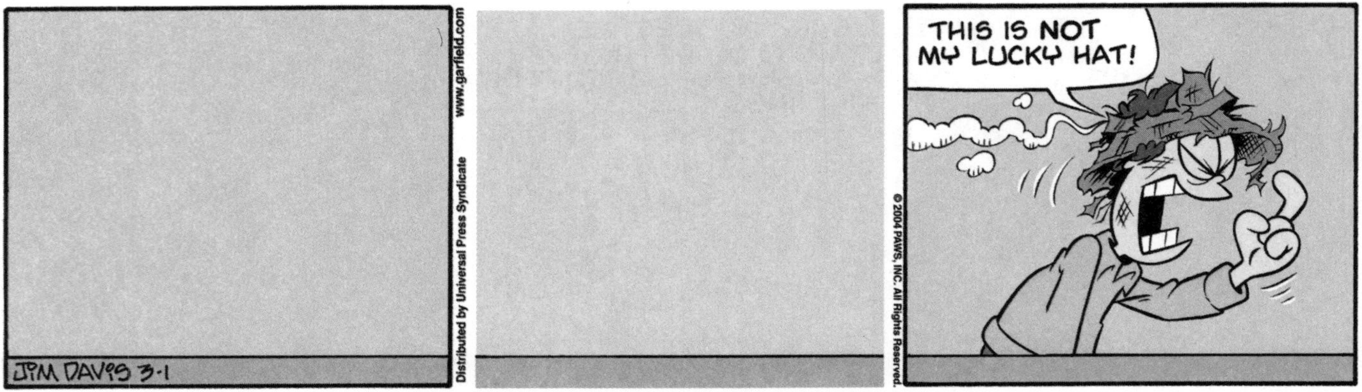
JIM DAVIS 3-1
Distributed by Universal Press Syndicate www.garfield.com
© 2004 PAWS, INC. All Rights Reserved.
THIS IS NOT MY LUCKY HAT!

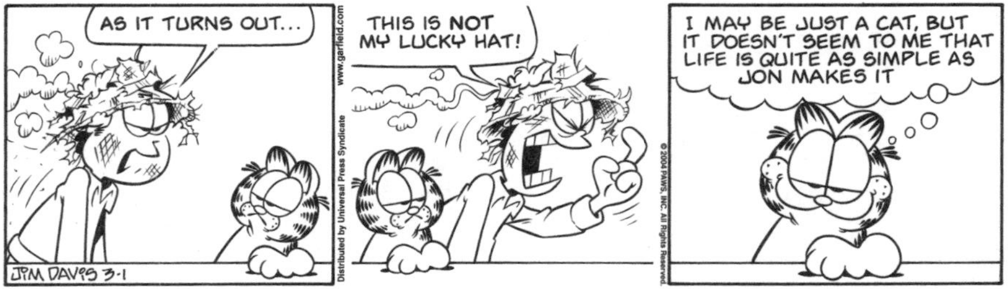
AS IT TURNS OUT...
JIM DAVIS 3-1
Distributed by Universal Press Syndicate www.garfield.com
THIS IS NOT MY LUCKY HAT!
© 2004 PAWS, INC. All Rights Reserved.
I MAY BE JUST A CAT, BUT IT DOESN'T SEEM TO ME THAT LIFE IS QUITE AS SIMPLE AS JON MAKES IT

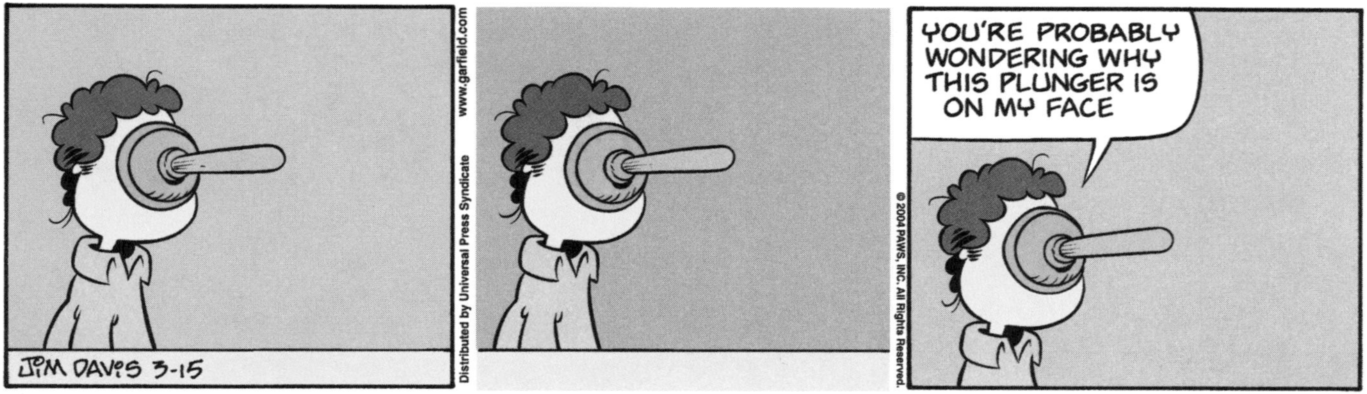
JIM DAVIS 3-15
www.garfield.com
Distributed by Universal Press Syndicate
© 2004 PAWS, INC. All Rights Reserved.
YOU'RE PROBABLY WONDERING WHY THIS PLUNGER IS ON MY FACE

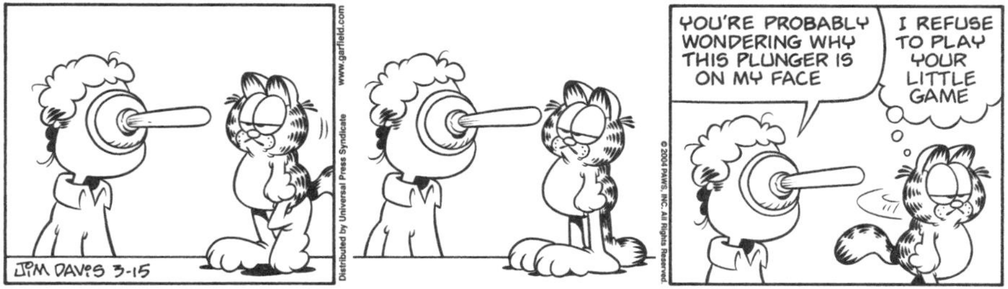
JIM DAVIS 3-15
www.garfield.com
Distributed by Universal Press Syndicate
YOU'RE PROBABLY WONDERING WHY THIS PLUNGER IS ON MY FACE
I REFUSE TO PLAY YOUR LITTLE GAME

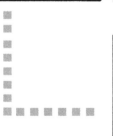

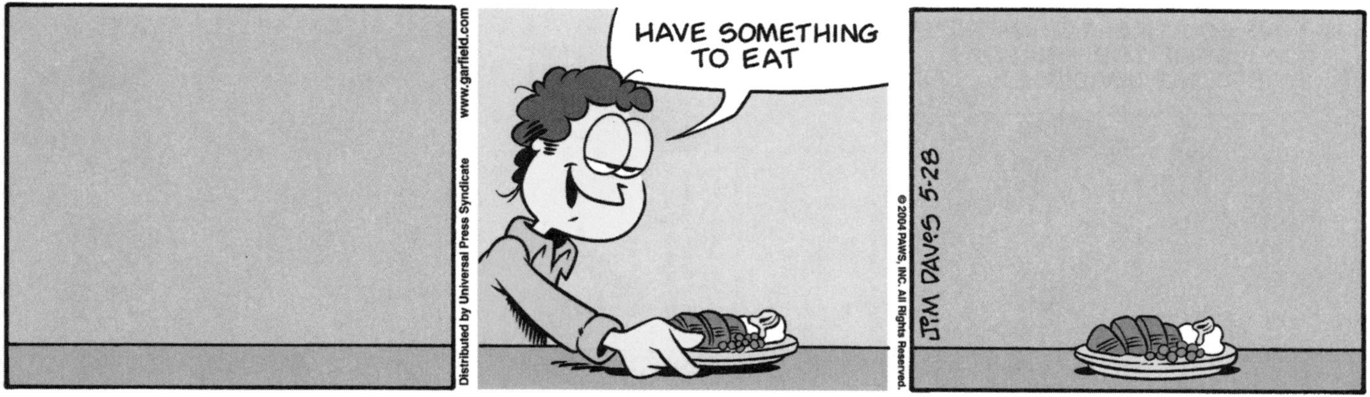
www.garfield.com
Distributed by Universal Press Syndicate
HAVE SOMETHING TO EAT
© 2004 PAWS, INC. All Rights Reserved.
JPM DAVPS 5-28

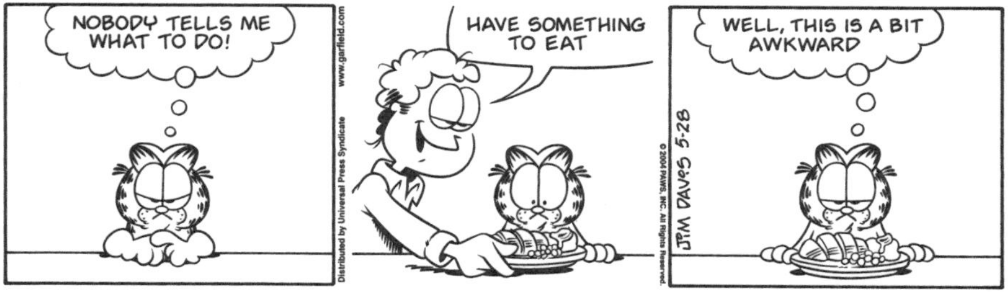
NOBODY TELLS ME WHAT TO DO!
www.garfield.com
Distributed by Universal Press Syndicate
HAVE SOMETHING TO EAT
© 2004 PAWS, INC. All Rights Reserved.
JPM DAVPS 5-28
WELL, THIS IS A BIT AWKWARD

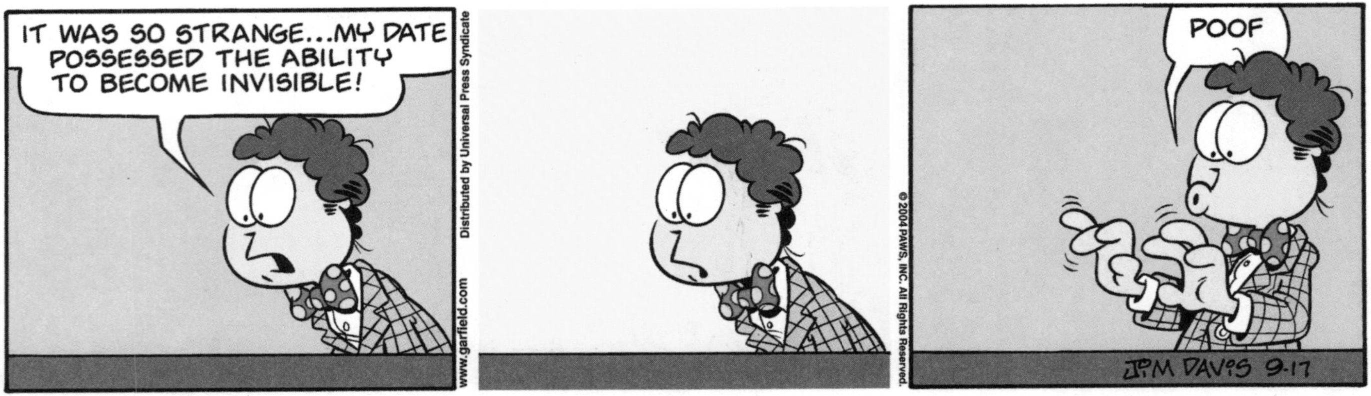
IT WAS SO STRANGE...MY DATE POSSESSED THE ABILITY TO BECOME INVISIBLE!
www.garfield.com Distributed by Universal Press Syndicate
© 2004 PAWS, INC. All Rights Reserved.
POOF
JIM DAVIS 9-17

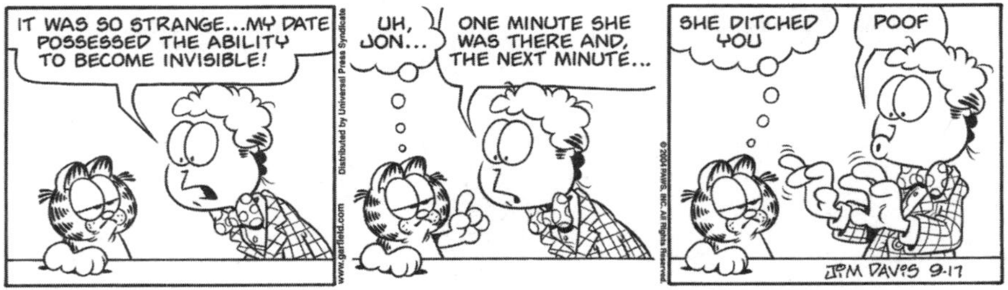
IT WAS SO STRANGE...MY DATE POSSESSED THE ABILITY TO BECOME INVISIBLE!
www.garfield.com Distributed by Universal Press Syndicate
UH, JON...
ONE MINUTE SHE WAS THERE AND, THE NEXT MINUTE...
© 2004 PAWS, INC. All Rights Reserved.
SHE DITCHED YOU
POOF
JIM DAVIS 9-17

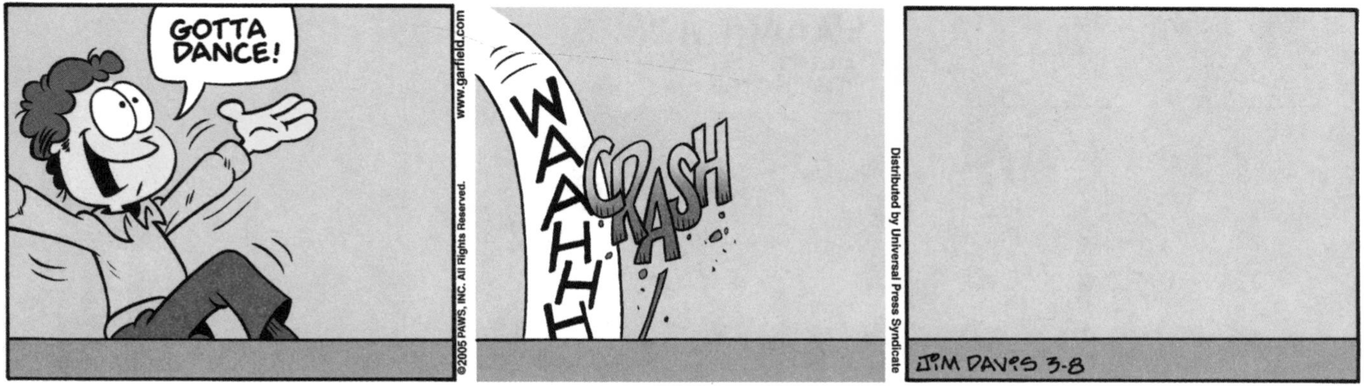
GOTTA DANCE!
©2005 PAWS, INC. All Rights Reserved. www.garfield.com
WAAHHH
CRASH
Distributed by Universal Press Syndicate
JIM DAVIS 3-8

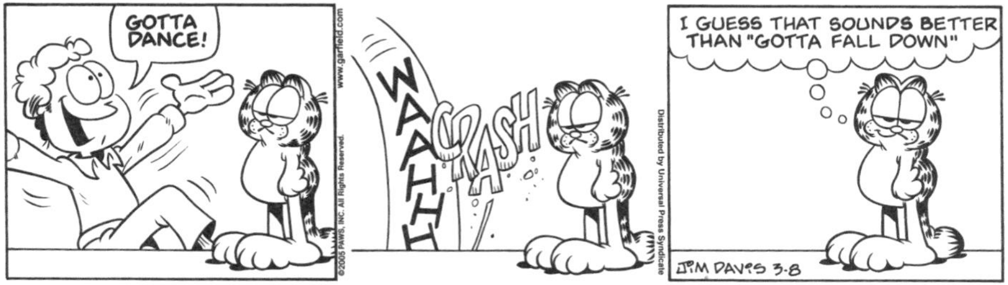
GOTTA DANCE!
WAAHHH
CRASH
I GUESS THAT SOUNDS BETTER THAN "GOTTA FALL DOWN"
JIM DAVIS 3-8

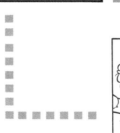

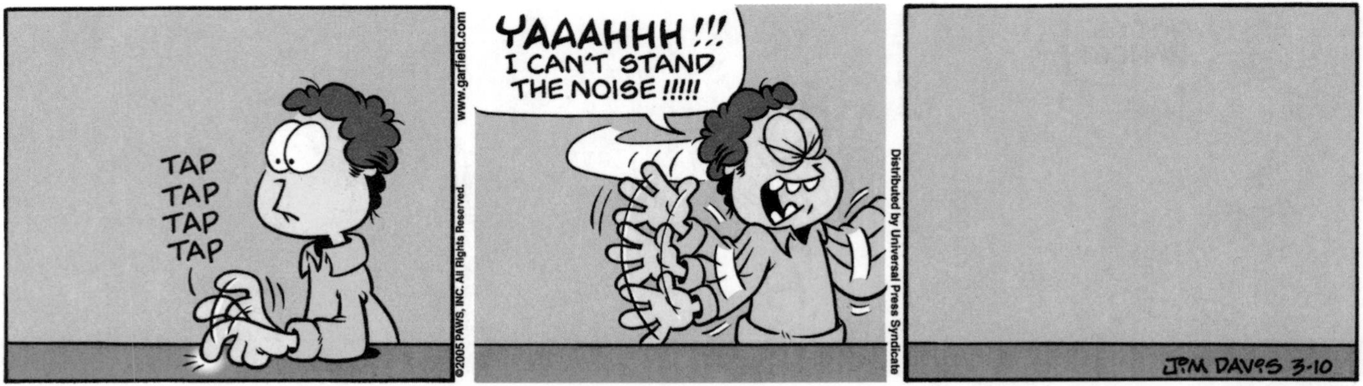
TAP
TAP
TAP
TAP
www.garfield.com
©2005 PAWS, INC. All Rights Reserved.
YAAAHHH !!!
I CAN'T STAND
THE NOISE !!!!!
Distributed by Universal Press Syndicate
JIM DAVIS 3-10

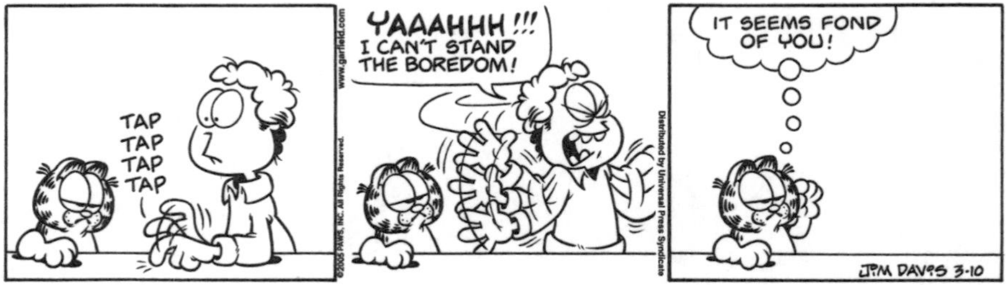
TAP
TAP
TAP
TAP
www.garfield.com
©2005 PAWS, INC. All Rights Reserved.
YAAAHHH !!!
I CAN'T STAND
THE BOREDOM!
Distributed by Universal Press Syndicate
IT SEEMS FOND
OF YOU!
JIM DAVIS 3-10

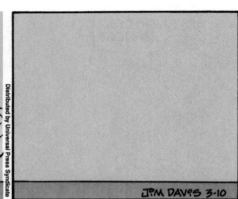

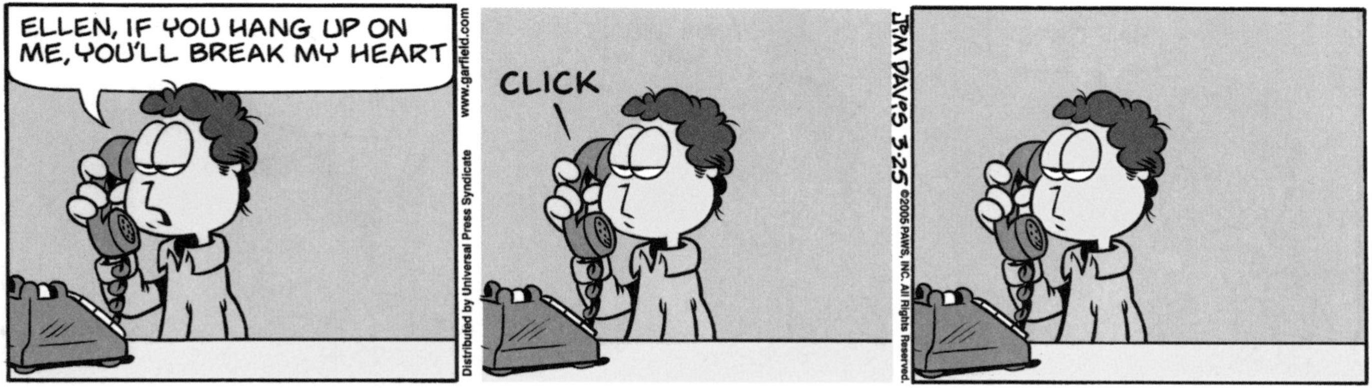
ELLEN, IF YOU HANG UP ON ME, YOU'LL BREAK MY HEART
www.garfield.com
Distributed by Universal Press Syndicate
CLICK
JIM DAVIS 3-25
©2005 PAWS, INC. All Rights Reserved.

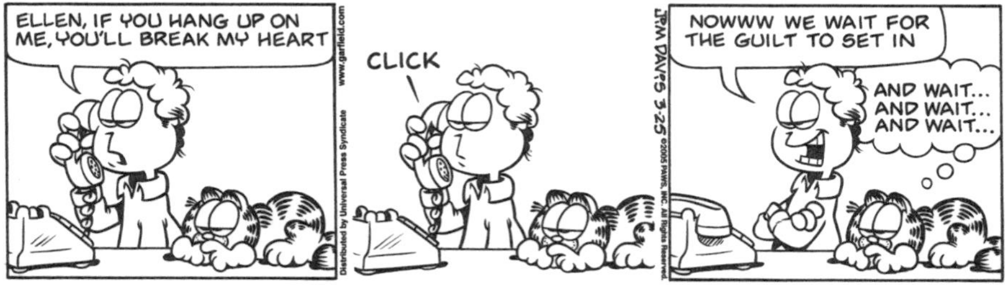
ELLEN, IF YOU HANG UP ON ME, YOU'LL BREAK MY HEART
www.garfield.com
Distributed by Universal Press Syndicate
CLICK
JIM DAVIS 3-25
NOWWW WE WAIT FOR THE GUILT TO SET IN
AND WAIT... AND WAIT... AND WAIT...

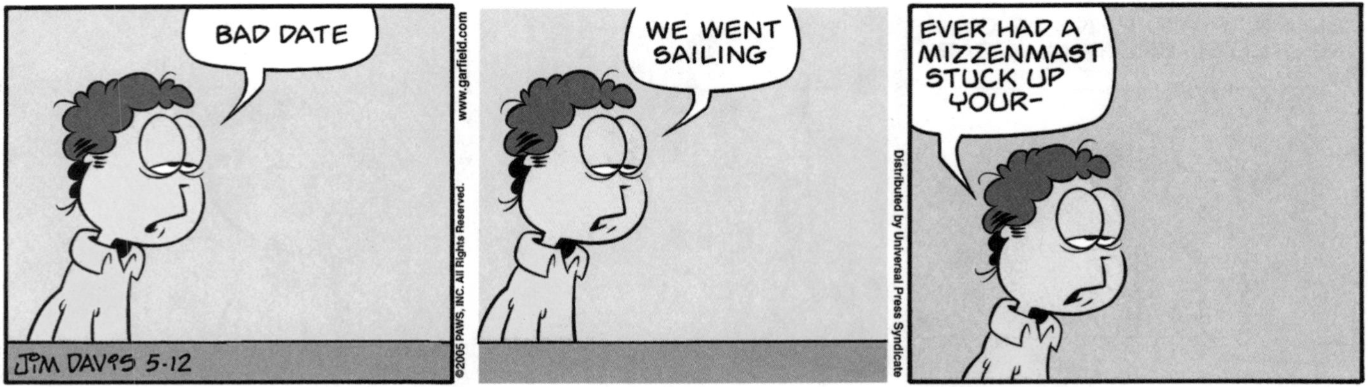
BAD DATE
JIM DAVIS 5-12
www.garfield.com
©2005 PAWS, INC. All Rights Reserved.
WE WENT SAILING
Distributed by Universal Press Syndicate
EVER HAD A MIZZENMAST STUCK UP YOUR-

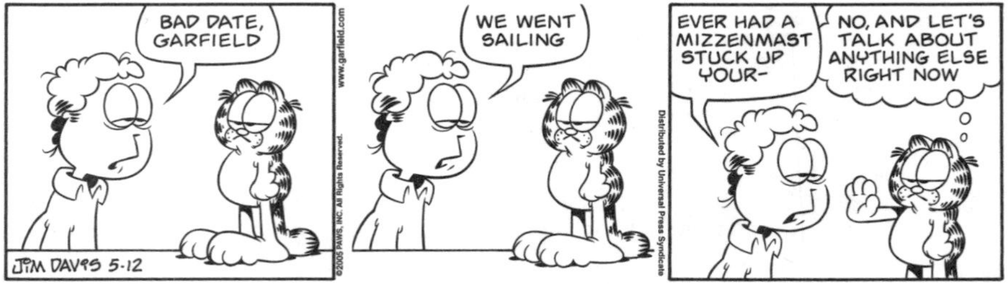
BAD DATE, GARFIELD
JIM DAVIS 5-12
www.garfield.com
©2005 PAWS, INC. All Rights Reserved.
WE WENT SAILING
Distributed by Universal Press Syndicate
EVER HAD A MIZZENMAST STUCK UP YOUR-
NO, AND LET'S TALK ABOUT ANYTHING ELSE RIGHT NOW

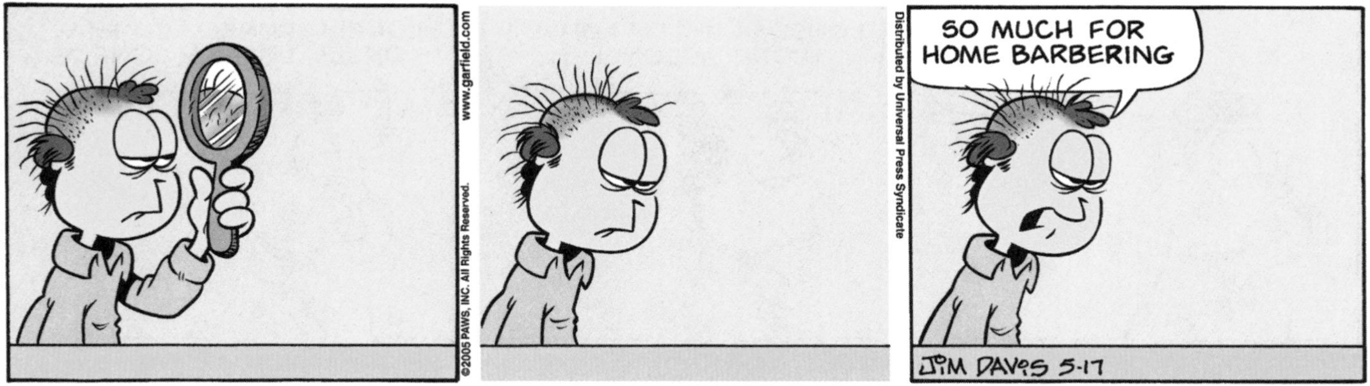
www.garfield.com
©2005 PAWS, INC. All Rights Reserved.
Distributed by Universal Press Syndicate
SO MUCH FOR HOME BARBERING
JIM DAVIS 5-17

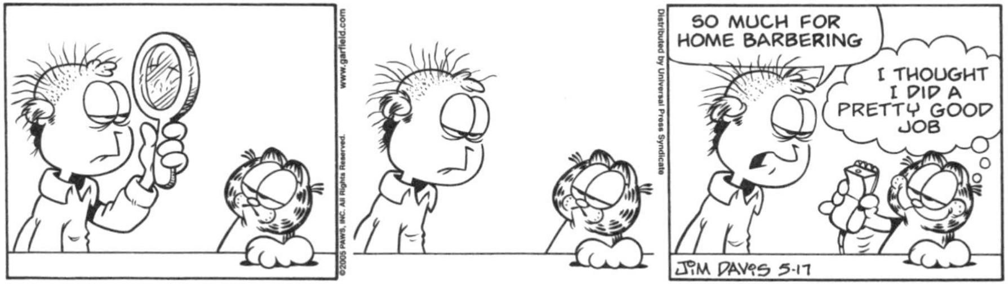
www.garfield.com
©2005 PAWS, INC. All Rights Reserved.
Distributed by Universal Press Syndicate
SO MUCH FOR HOME BARBERING
I THOUGHT I DID A PRETTY GOOD JOB
JIM DAVIS 5-17

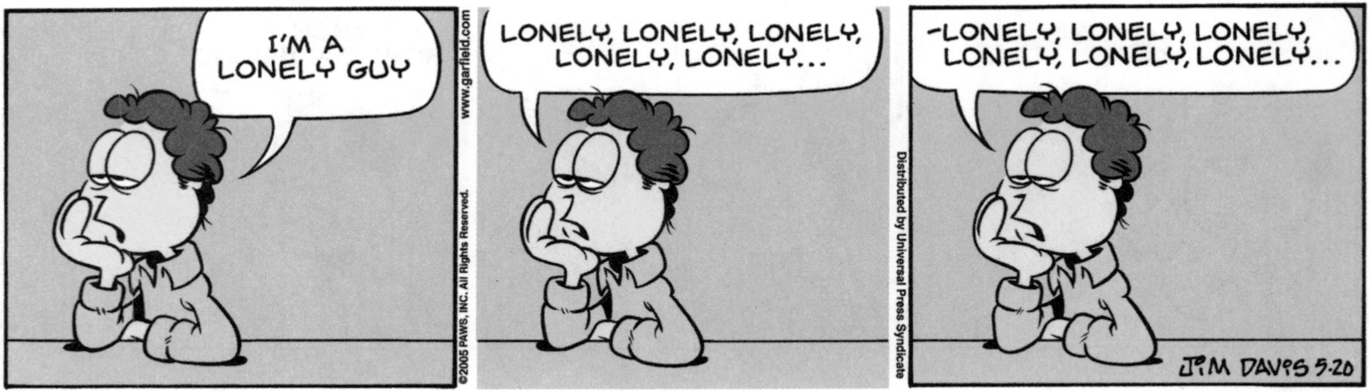
I'M A LONELY GUY
LONELY, LONELY, LONELY, LONELY, LONELY...
-LONELY, LONELY, LONELY, LONELY, LONELY, LONELY...
©2005 PAWS, INC. All Rights Reserved.
www.garfield.com
Distributed by Universal Press Syndicate
JIM DAVIS 5-20

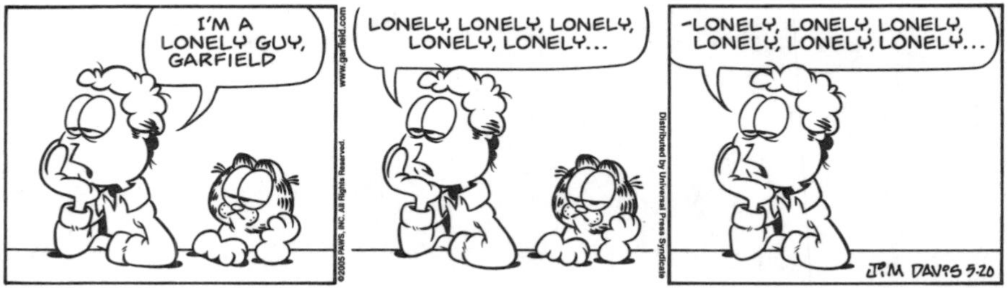
I'M A LONELY GUY, GARFIELD
LONELY, LONELY, LONELY, LONELY, LONELY...
-LONELY, LONELY, LONELY, LONELY, LONELY, LONELY...
©2005 PAWS, INC. All Rights Reserved.
www.garfield.com
Distributed by Universal Press Syndicate
JIM DAVIS 5-20

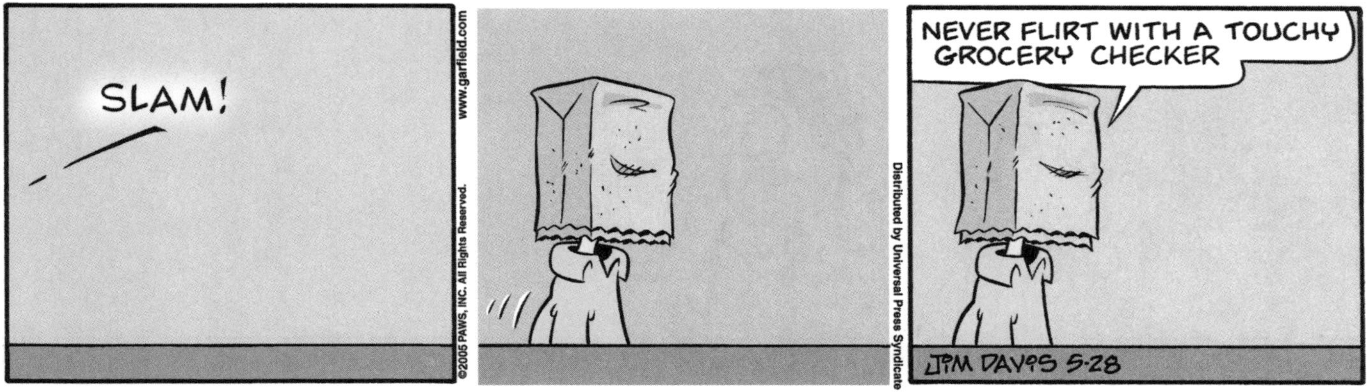
SLAM!
©2005 PAWS, INC. All Rights Reserved. www.garfield.com
Distributed by Universal Press Syndicate
NEVER FLIRT WITH A TOUCHY GROCERY CHECKER
JIM DAVIS 5-28

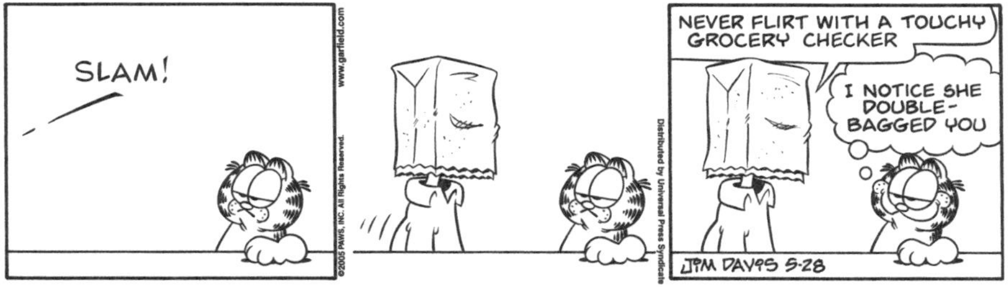
SLAM!
©2005 PAWS, INC. All Rights Reserved. www.garfield.com
Distributed by Universal Press Syndicate
NEVER FLIRT WITH A TOUCHY GROCERY CHECKER
I NOTICE SHE DOUBLE-BAGGED YOU
JIM DAVIS 5-28

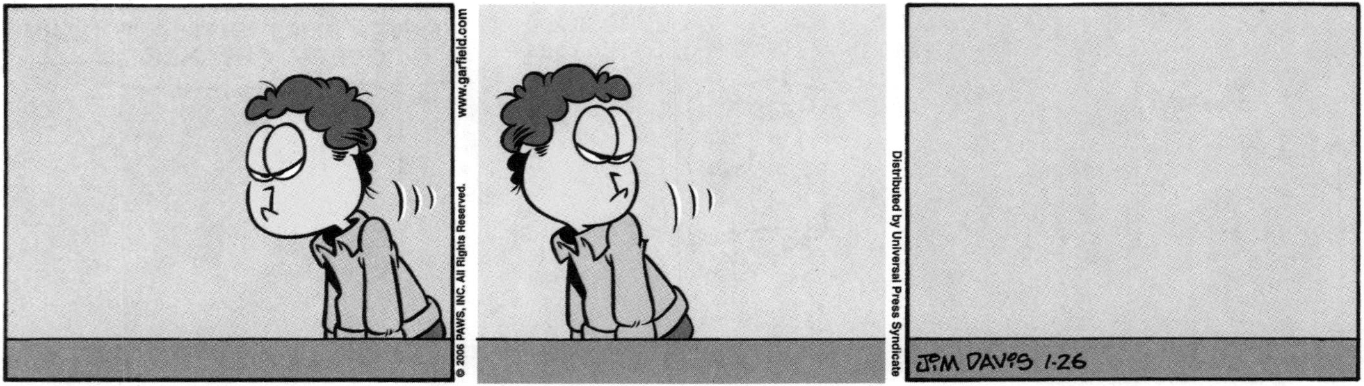
© 2006 PAWS, INC. All Rights Reserved. www.garfield.com
Distributed by Universal Press Syndicate
JIM DAVIS 1-26

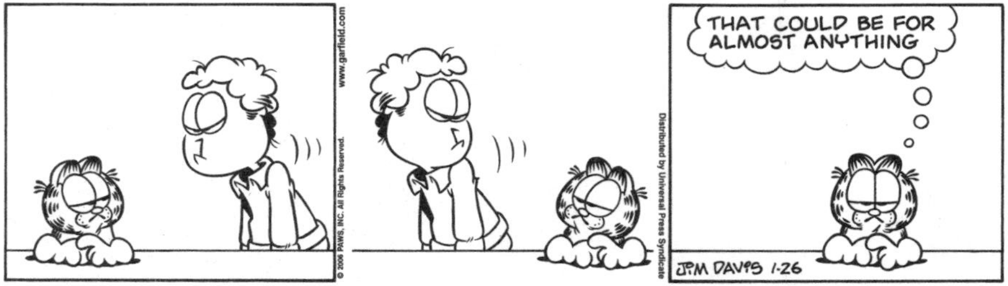
© 2006 PAWS, INC. All Rights Reserved. www.garfield.com
Distributed by Universal Press Syndicate
THAT COULD BE FOR ALMOST ANYTHING
JIM DAVIS 1-26

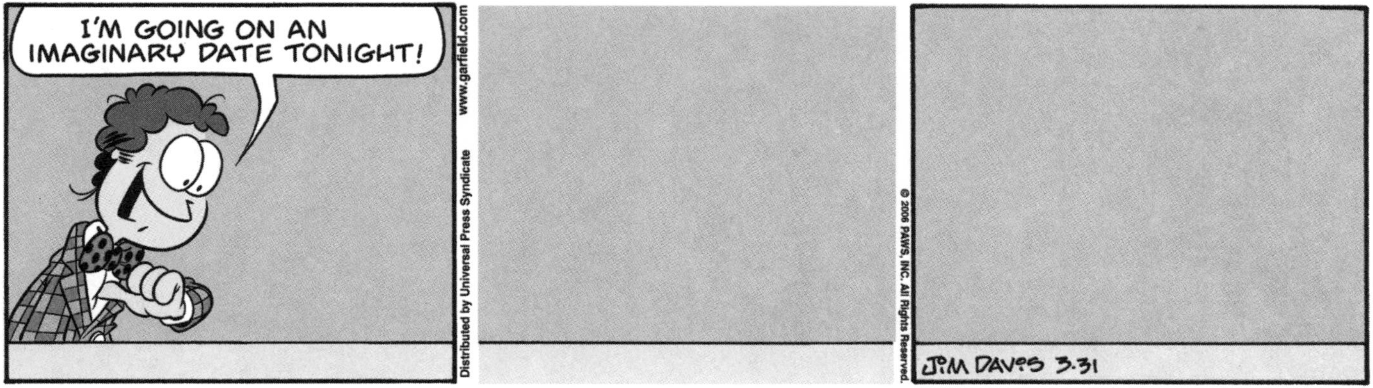
I'M GOING ON AN IMAGINARY DATE TONIGHT!
www.garfield.com
Distributed by Universal Press Syndicate
© 2006 PAWS, INC. All Rights Reserved.
JIM DAVIS 3.31

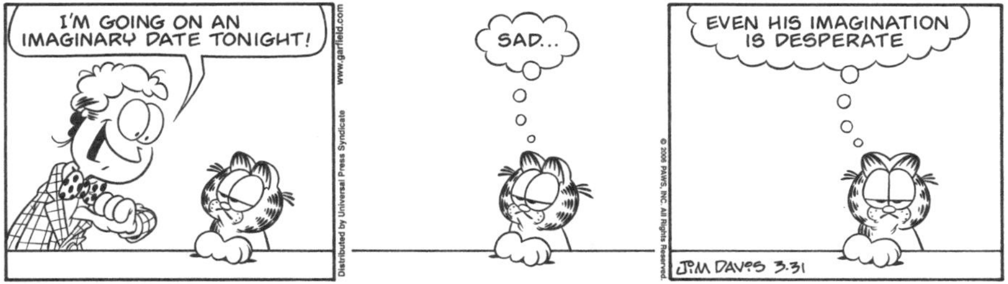
I'M GOING ON AN IMAGINARY DATE TONIGHT!
www.garfield.com
Distributed by Universal Press Syndicate
SAD...
© 2006 PAWS, INC. All Rights Reserved.
EVEN HIS IMAGINATION IS DESPERATE
JIM DAVIS 3.31

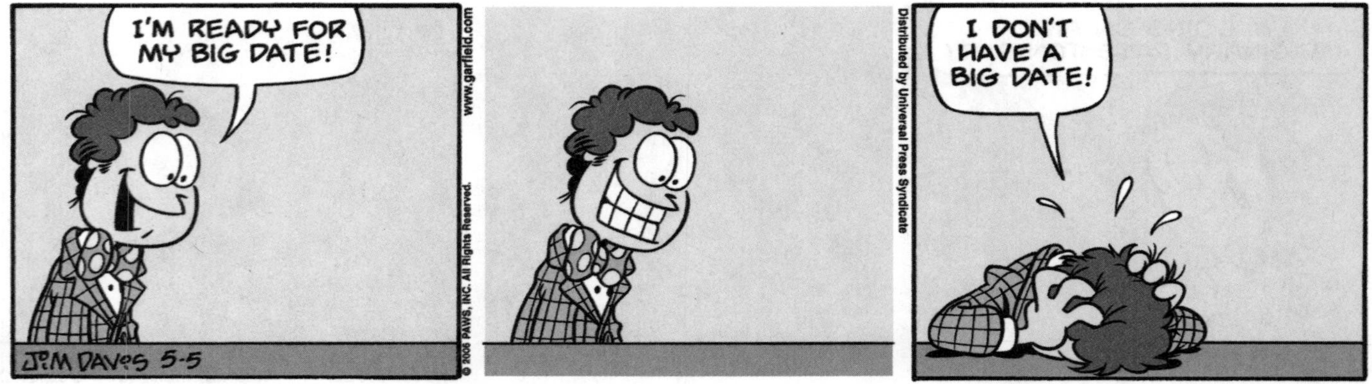
I'M READY FOR MY BIG DATE!
JIM DAVIS 5-5
© 2006 PAWS, INC. All Rights Reserved. www.garfield.com
Distributed by Universal Press Syndicate
I DON'T HAVE A BIG DATE!

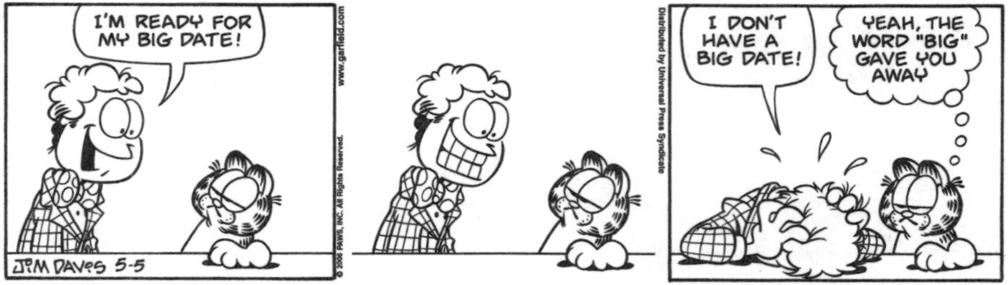
I'M READY FOR MY BIG DATE!
JIM DAVIS 5-5
© 2006 PAWS, INC. All Rights Reserved. www.garfield.com
Distributed by Universal Press Syndicate
I DON'T HAVE A BIG DATE!
YEAH, THE WORD "BIG" GAVE YOU AWAY

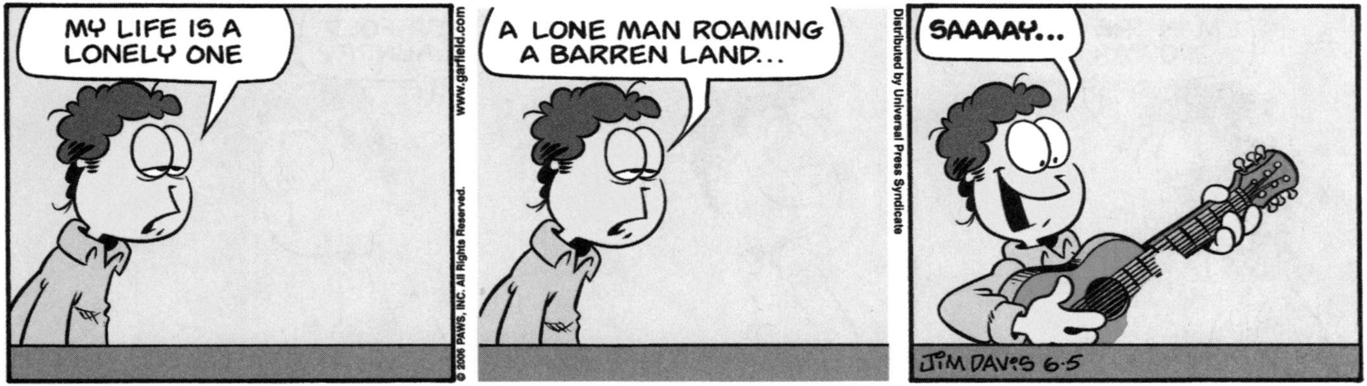
MY LIFE IS A LONELY ONE
www.garfield.com
© 2006 PAWS, INC. All Rights Reserved.
A LONE MAN ROAMING A BARREN LAND...
Distributed by Universal Press Syndicate
SAAAAY...
JIM DAVIS 6·5

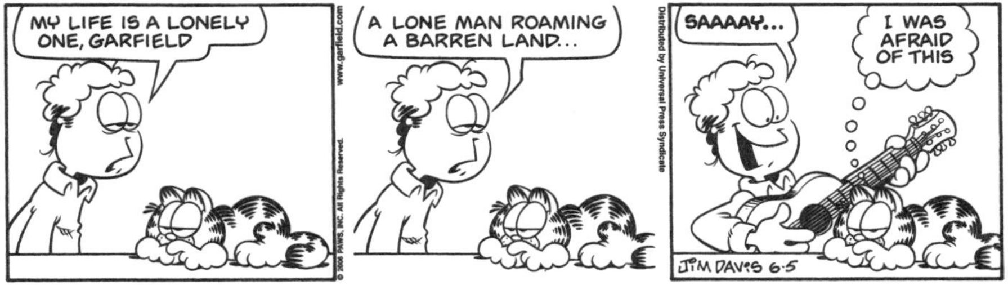
MY LIFE IS A LONELY ONE, GARFIELD
A LONE MAN ROAMING A BARREN LAND...
SAAAAY...
I WAS AFRAID OF THIS
JIM DAVIS 6·5

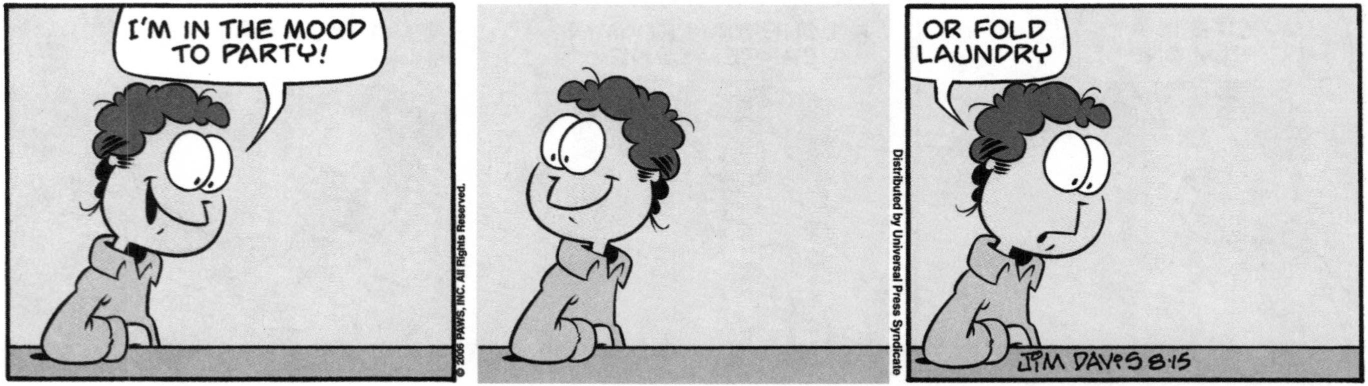
I'M IN THE MOOD TO PARTY!
OR FOLD LAUNDRY
JIM DAVIS 8·15
© 2006 PAWS, INC. All Rights Reserved.
Distributed by Universal Press Syndicate

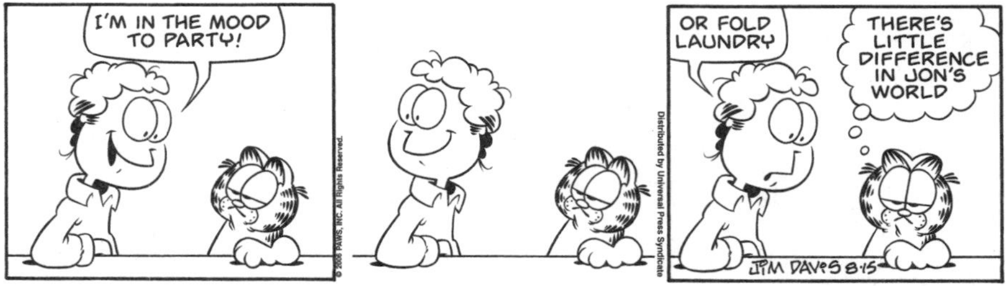
I'M IN THE MOOD TO PARTY!
OR FOLD LAUNDRY
THERE'S LITTLE DIFFERENCE IN JON'S WORLD
JIM DAVIS 8·15

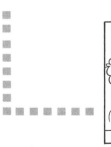

87

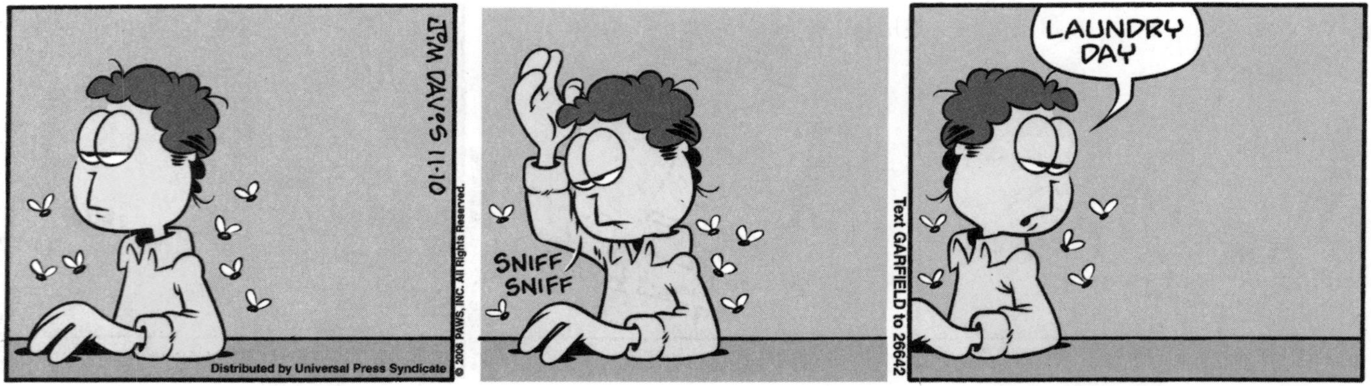
JPM DAVIS 11-10
© 2006 PAWS, INC. All Rights Reserved.
Distributed by Universal Press Syndicate
SNIFF SNIFF
Text GARFIELD to 26642
LAUNDRY DAY

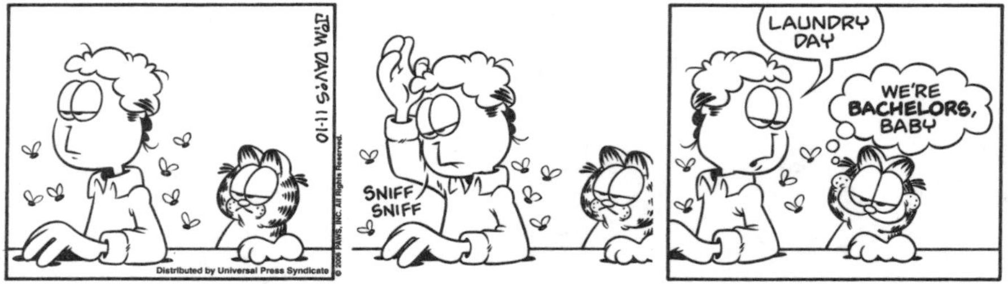
JPM DAVIS 11-10
Distributed by Universal Press Syndicate
SNIFF SNIFF
LAUNDRY DAY
WE'RE BACHELORS, BABY

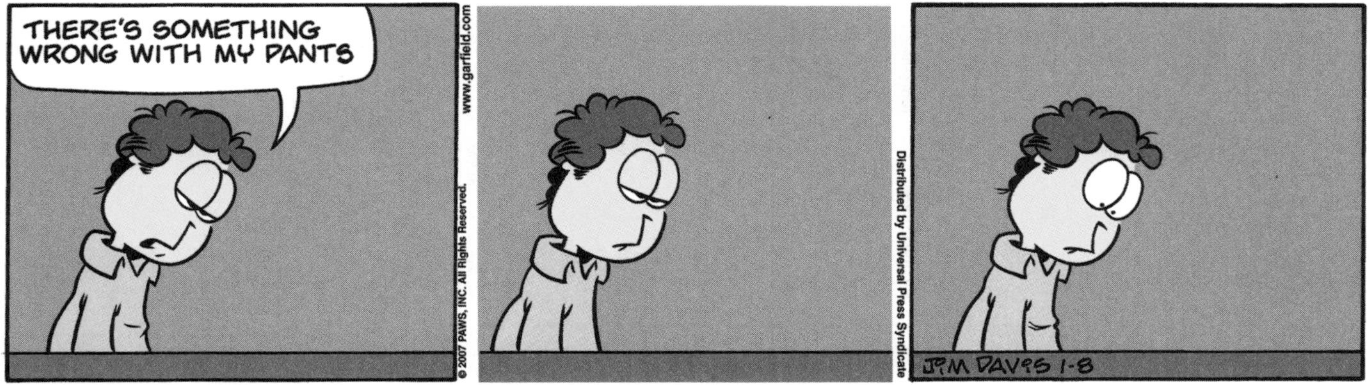
THERE'S SOMETHING WRONG WITH MY PANTS
© 2007 PAWS, INC. All Rights Reserved.
www.garfield.com
Distributed by Universal Press Syndicate
JIM DAVIS 1-8

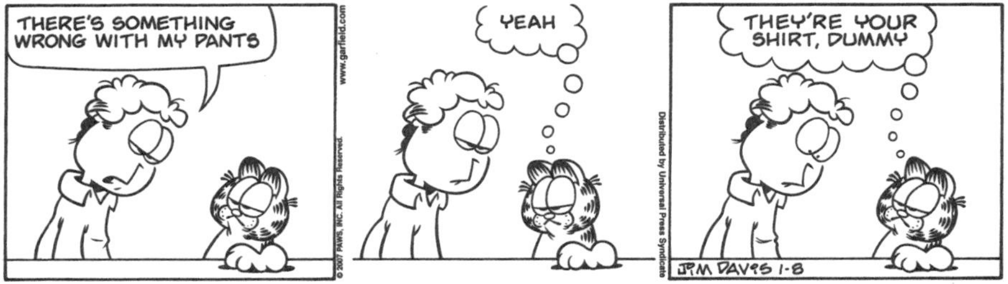
THERE'S SOMETHING WRONG WITH MY PANTS
© 2007 PAWS, INC. All Rights Reserved.
www.garfield.com
YEAH
Distributed by Universal Press Syndicate
THEY'RE YOUR SHIRT, DUMMY
JIM DAVIS 1-8

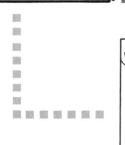

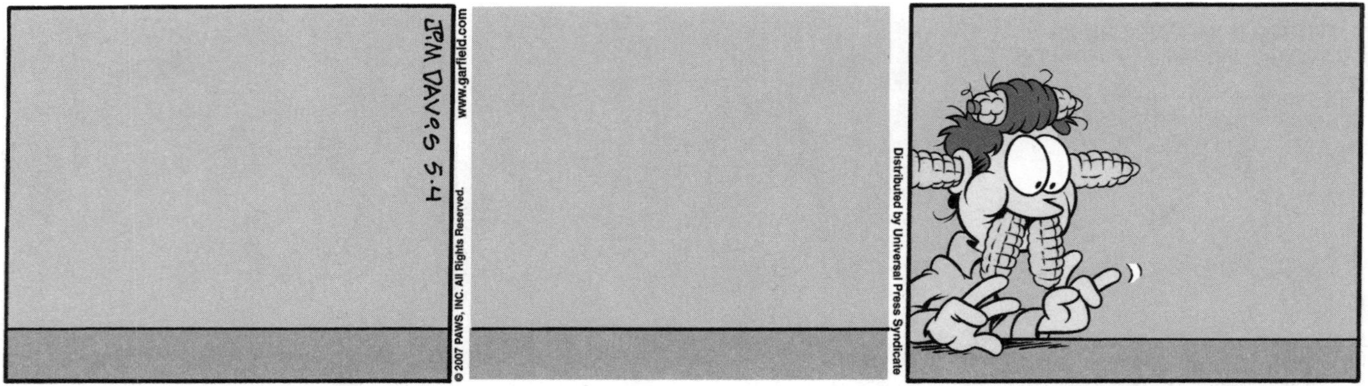
www.garfield.com
© 2007 PAWS, INC. All Rights Reserved.
Distributed by Universal Press Syndicate

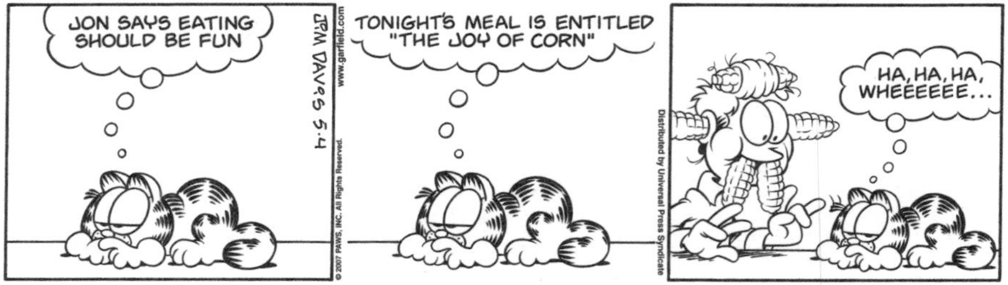
JON SAYS EATING SHOULD BE FUN
www.garfield.com
© 2007 PAWS, INC. All Rights Reserved.
TONIGHT'S MEAL IS ENTITLED "THE JOY OF CORN"
Distributed by Universal Press Syndicate
HA, HA, HA, WHEEEEEE...

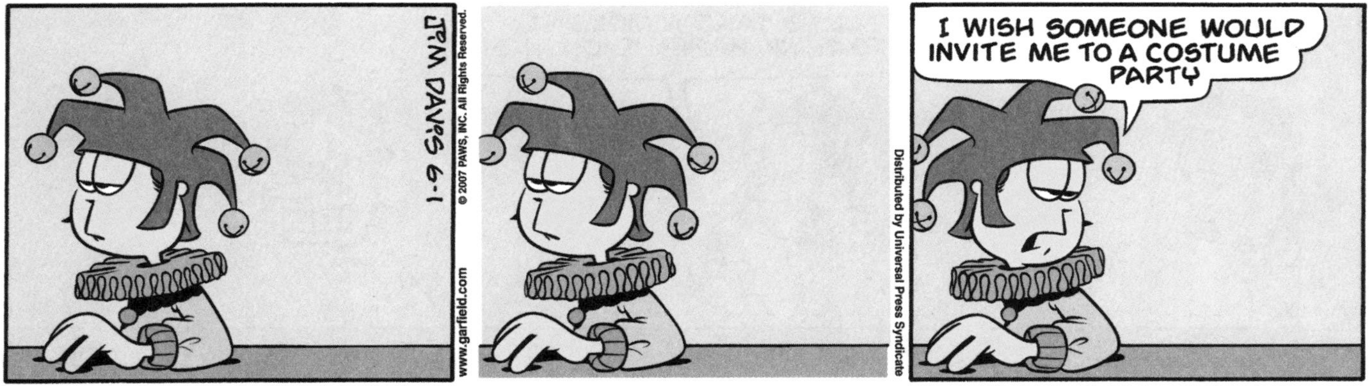
JPM DAVPS 6-1
© 2007 PAWS, INC. All Rights Reserved.
www.garfield.com
Distributed by Universal Press Syndicate
I WISH SOMEONE WOULD INVITE ME TO A COSTUME PARTY

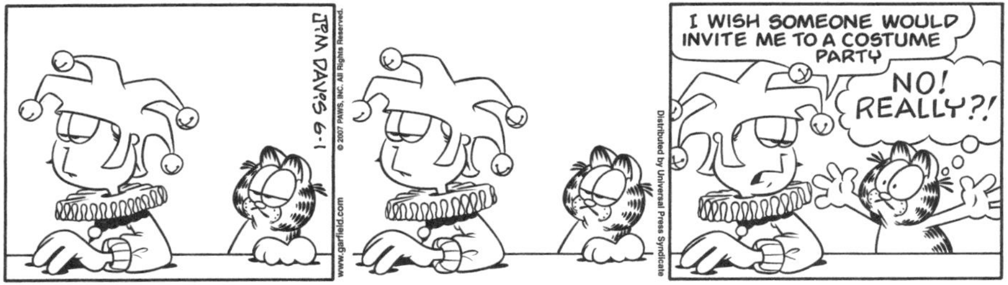
JPM DAVPS 6-1
© 2007 PAWS, INC. All Rights Reserved.
www.garfield.com
Distributed by Universal Press Syndicate
I WISH SOMEONE WOULD INVITE ME TO A COSTUME PARTY
NO! REALLY?!

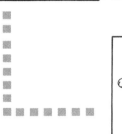

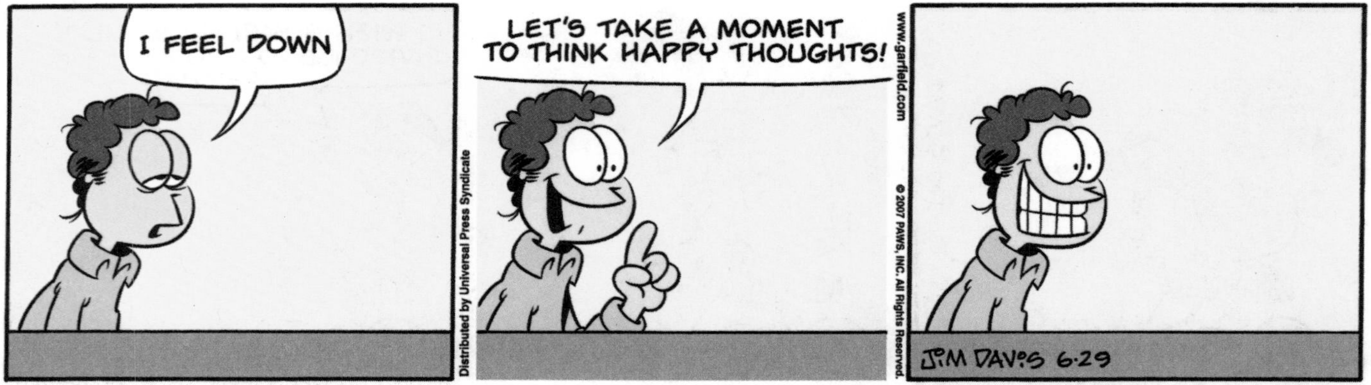
I FEEL DOWN
LET'S TAKE A MOMENT TO THINK HAPPY THOUGHTS!
Distributed by Universal Press Syndicate
www.garfield.com
© 2007 PAWS, INC. All Rights Reserved.
JIM DAVIS 6·29

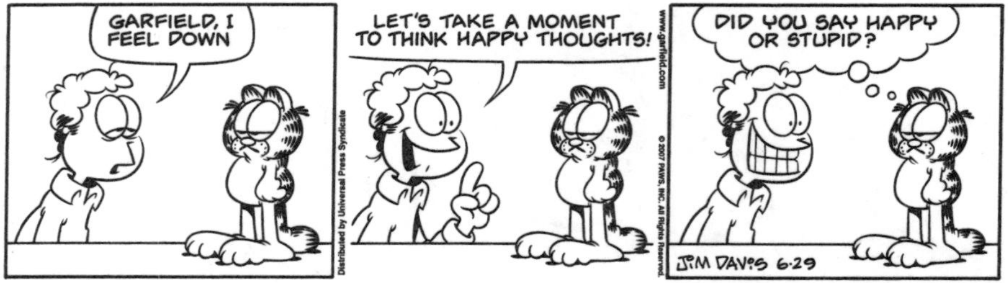
GARFIELD, I FEEL DOWN
LET'S TAKE A MOMENT TO THINK HAPPY THOUGHTS!
DID YOU SAY HAPPY OR STUPID?
JIM DAVIS 6·29

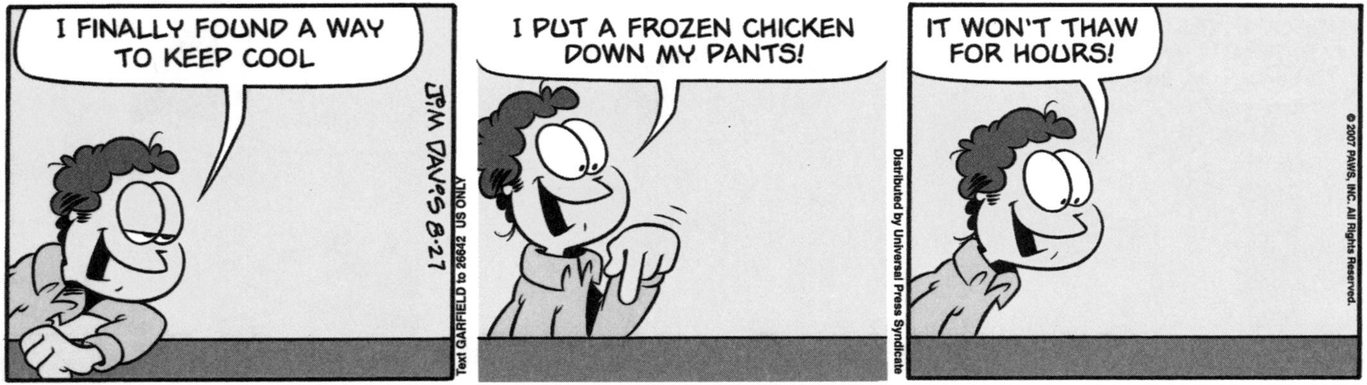
I FINALLY FOUND A WAY TO KEEP COOL
JIM DAVIS 8-27
Text GARFIELD to 26642 US ONLY
I PUT A FROZEN CHICKEN DOWN MY PANTS!
Distributed by Universal Press Syndicate
IT WON'T THAW FOR HOURS!
© 2007 PAWS, INC. All Rights Reserved.

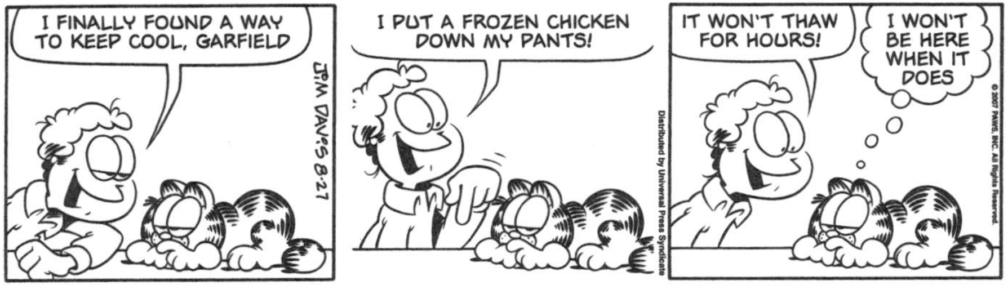
I FINALLY FOUND A WAY TO KEEP COOL, GARFIELD
JIM DAVIS 8-27
I PUT A FROZEN CHICKEN DOWN MY PANTS!
Distributed by Universal Press Syndicate
IT WON'T THAW FOR HOURS!
I WON'T BE HERE WHEN IT DOES
© 2007 PAWS, INC. All Rights Reserved.

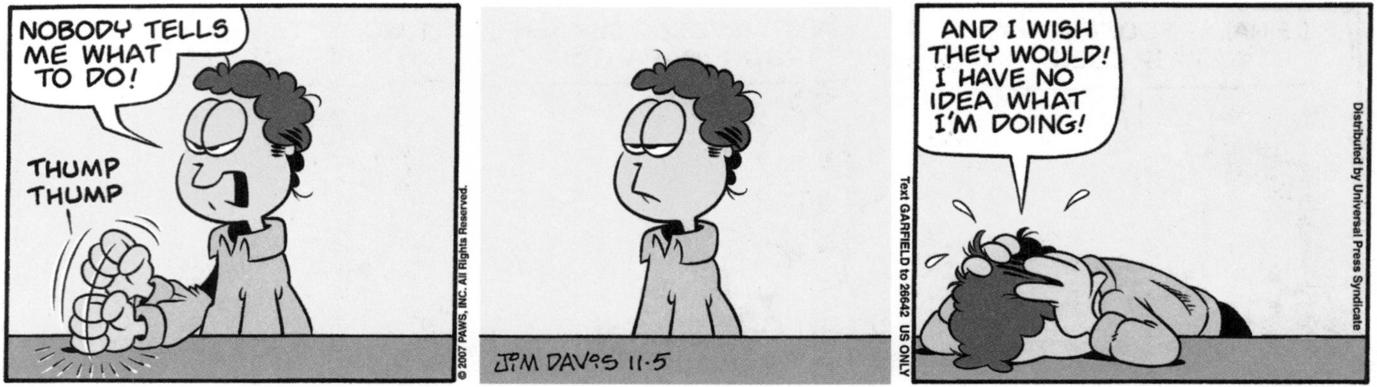
NOBODY TELLS ME WHAT TO DO!
THUMP THUMP
© 2007 PAWS, INC. All Rights Reserved.
JIM DAVIS 11·5
Text GARFIELD to 26642 US ONLY
AND I WISH THEY WOULD! I HAVE NO IDEA WHAT I'M DOING!
Distributed by Universal Press Syndicate

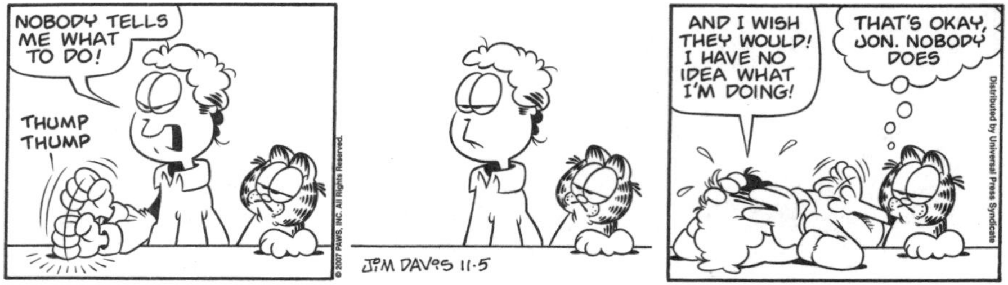
NOBODY TELLS ME WHAT TO DO!
THUMP THUMP
© 2007 PAWS, INC. All Rights Reserved.
JIM DAVIS 11·5
AND I WISH THEY WOULD! I HAVE NO IDEA WHAT I'M DOING!
THAT'S OKAY, JON. NOBODY DOES
Distributed by Universal Press Syndicate

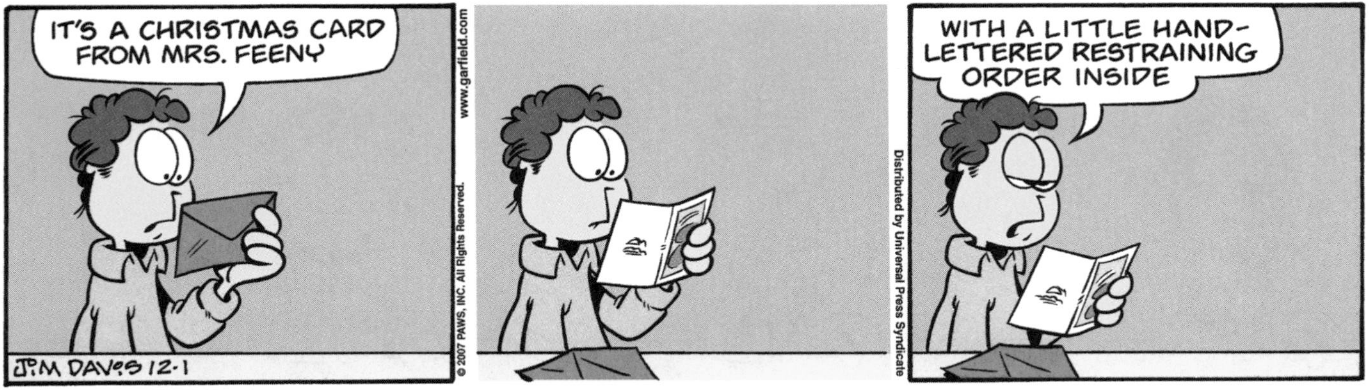
IT'S A CHRISTMAS CARD FROM MRS. FEENY
WITH A LITTLE HAND-LETTERED RESTRAINING ORDER INSIDE
JIM DAVIS 12-1

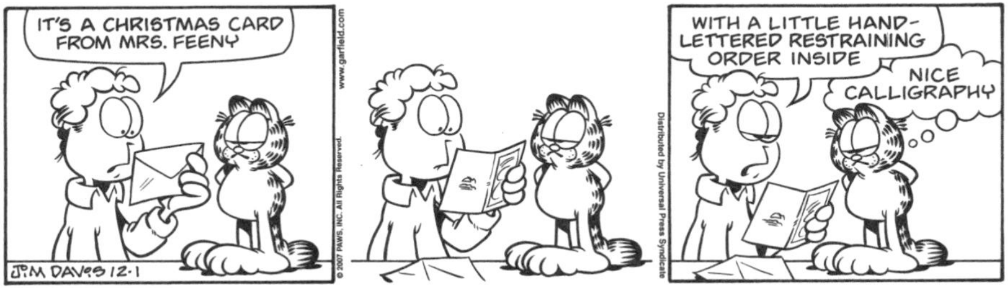
IT'S A CHRISTMAS CARD FROM MRS. FEENY
WITH A LITTLE HAND-LETTERED RESTRAINING ORDER INSIDE
NICE CALLIGRAPHY

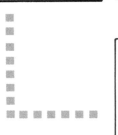

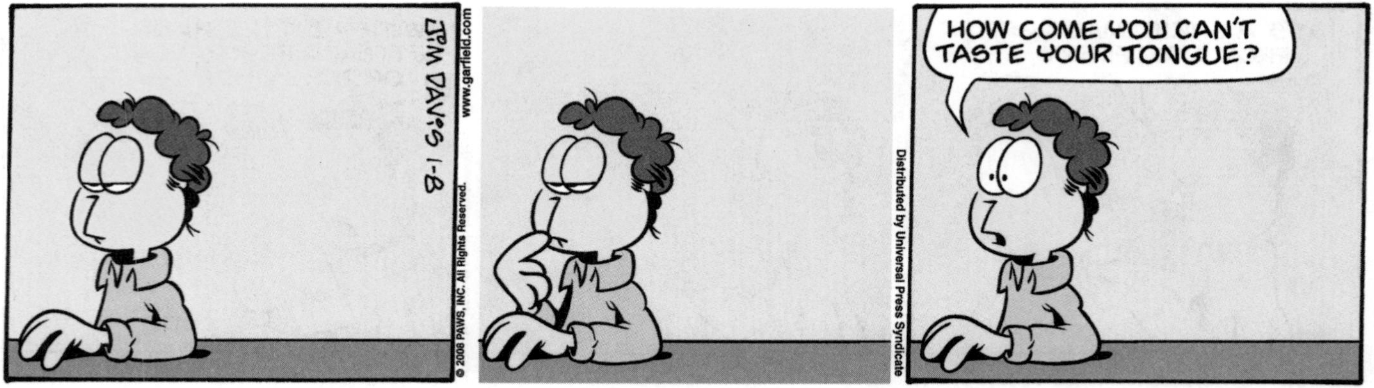
JIM DAVIS 1-8
www.garfield.com
© 2008 PAWS, INC. All Rights Reserved.
Distributed by Universal Press Syndicate
HOW COME YOU CAN'T TASTE YOUR TONGUE?

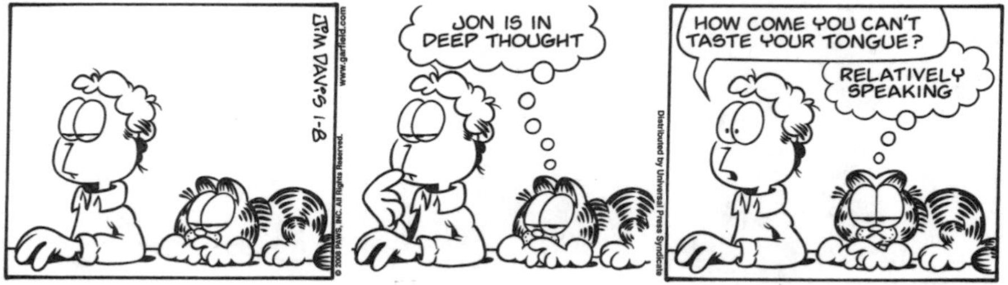
JIM DAVIS 1-8
www.garfield.com
JON IS IN DEEP THOUGHT
HOW COME YOU CAN'T TASTE YOUR TONGUE?
RELATIVELY SPEAKING

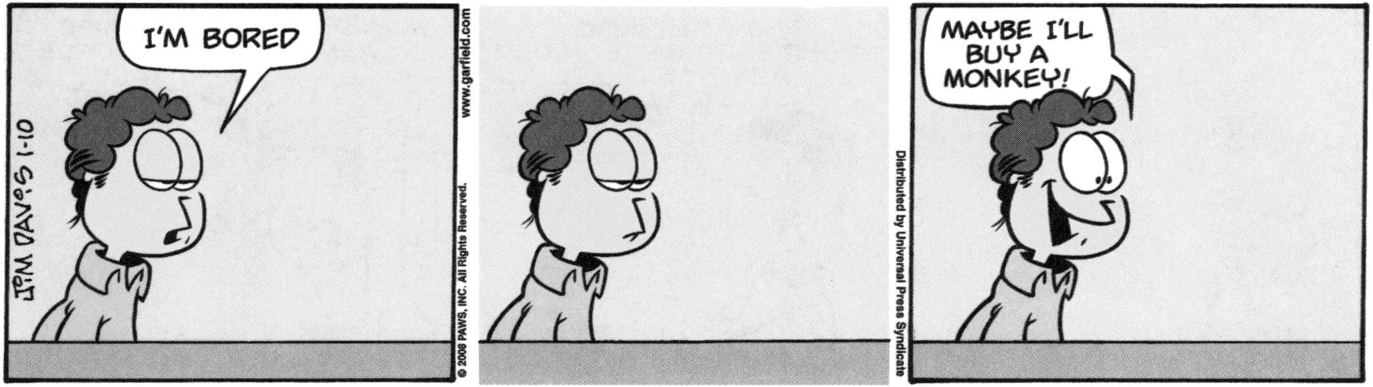
I'M BORED
MAYBE I'LL BUY A MONKEY!
www.garfield.com
© 2008 PAWS, INC. All Rights Reserved.
Distributed by Universal Press Syndicate

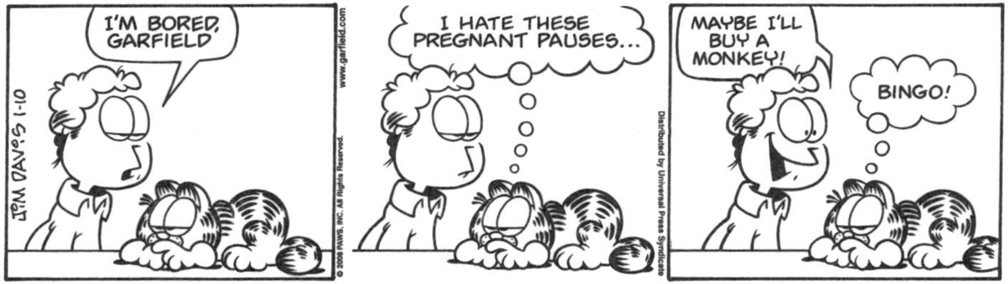
I'M BORED, GARFIELD
I HATE THESE PREGNANT PAUSES...
MAYBE I'LL BUY A MONKEY!
BINGO!

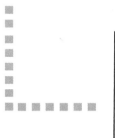

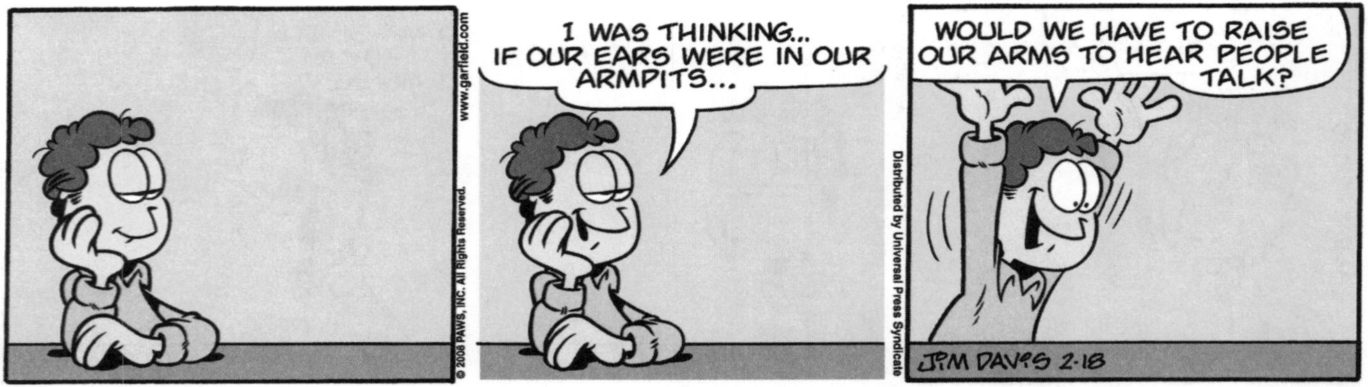
www.garfield.com
© 2008 PAWS, INC. All Rights Reserved.
I WAS THINKING...
IF OUR EARS WERE IN OUR ARMPITS...
Distributed by Universal Press Syndicate
WOULD WE HAVE TO RAISE OUR ARMS TO HEAR PEOPLE TALK?
JIM DAVIS 2-18

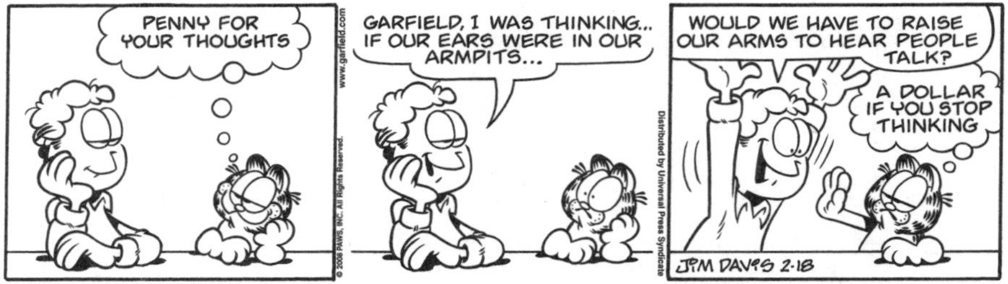
PENNY FOR YOUR THOUGHTS
www.garfield.com
© 2008 PAWS, INC. All Rights Reserved.
GARFIELD, I WAS THINKING... IF OUR EARS WERE IN OUR ARMPITS...
Distributed by Universal Press Syndicate
WOULD WE HAVE TO RAISE OUR ARMS TO HEAR PEOPLE TALK?
A DOLLAR IF YOU STOP THINKING
JIM DAVIS 2-18

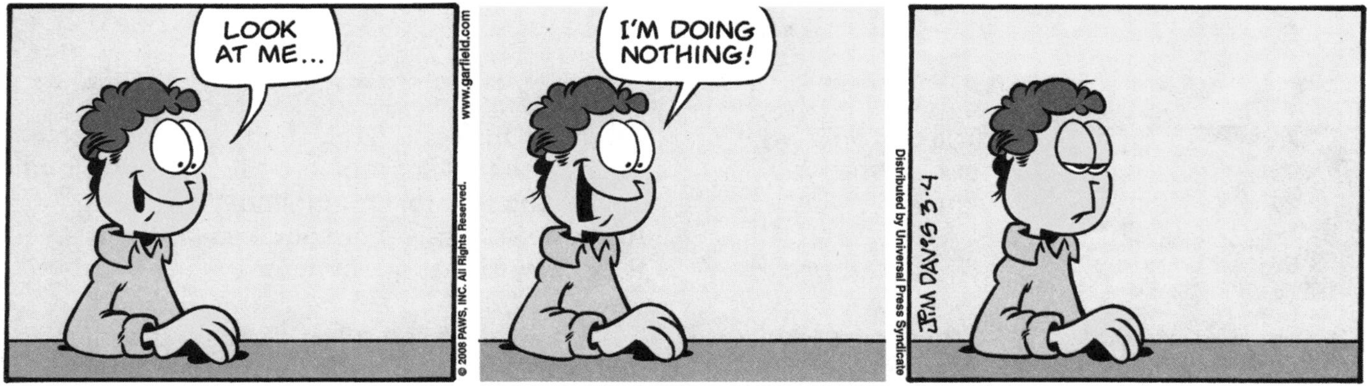
LOOK AT ME...
I'M DOING NOTHING!
© 2008 PAWS, INC. All Rights Reserved. www.garfield.com
Distributed by Universal Press Syndicate

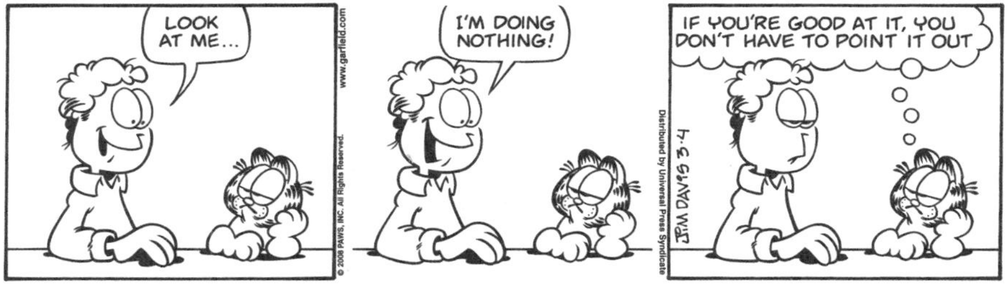
LOOK AT ME...
I'M DOING NOTHING!
IF YOU'RE GOOD AT IT, YOU DON'T HAVE TO POINT IT OUT

A Word from Jim Davis

You can only write about what you know. . . .

I'm Jon Arbuckle.

When I was a kid there was a coffee commercial on TV that said, "Jon Arbuckle says this coffee is really great!" or something like that.

I never knew who Jon Arbuckle was, and neither did anyone else. So, in college, I started dropping Jon Arbuckle's name when I needed to lend credibility to something. In a student senate debate I once said, "Noted educator and theologian Jon Arbuckle once said, 'Education, for education's sake, often falls short of its goals.' " At that point I heard the senators mumbling, "Aaaah, Jon Arbuckle" and saw them nod knowingly as if they'd heard that quote before.

When I write for Jon, all I have to do is conjure up my college dating days. I was the fraternity strikeout king! It's hard to say why I had so much trouble getting dates; primarily because there were so many reasons. I always waited until the last minute to call anyone. Who knows when there would be a hot game of double-deck euchre starting in the card room? I could never afford to take a girl out on a real date (like one with food). In a day of bell-bottoms, I still sported jeans with a six-inch peg. Accessorize that with a bright red Ban Lon shirt and matching Hush

Puppies (avec red socks), and, well, you get a reputation. . . . But, darn it, you gotta love Jon/me, because I/Jon always look on the bright side of things. Don Quixote said it best, "Tomorrow will be a new day." And who doesn't love Clark Griswold from the Vacation movie series? This guy could find the bright side of a dead Aunt Edna in the backseat and a Dinkyless dog leash tied to the back bumper of his car! There's a message here, people! . . . And Jon has no idea what that message is . . . and neither do I . . . and neither do Clark and Don. We just live it, and it feels pretty good.

With that said, someone sent me a link to Garfield Minus Garfield one day, and I was immediately struck by the simplicity and the honesty of the concept. Essentially, Garfield does the color commentary on Jon's hapless existence. Strip away Garfield's superfluous comments, and you're left with the stark reality of Jon's bleak circumstances: Without Garfield it's more com-forting in a lefthanded sort of way. More often than not when we laugh at a gag, it isn't because it's funny; it's because we're thinking, "Isn't that true."

We realize that we aren't the only insecure people on the planet after reading Garfield Minus Garfield. And loneliness? Who could be lonelier than Jon Arbuckle? How comforting. I guess loneliness loves company. . . .

Dan Walsh's variation on Garfield was so much fun I had to do a few for myself.

Thanks, Dan, for fashioning a fresh approach to my old feature.

Enjoy!

Jim Davis

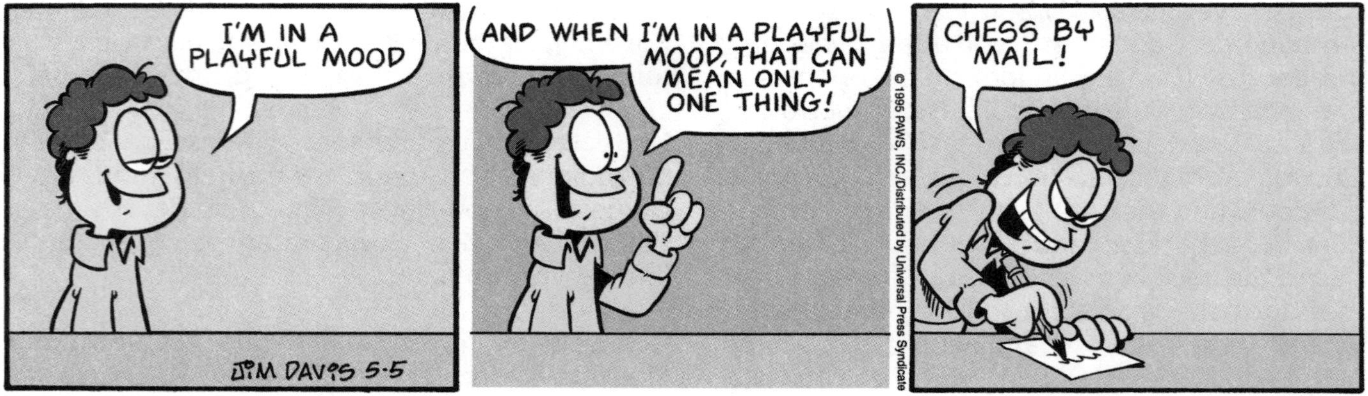
I'M IN A PLAYFUL MOOD
JIM DAVIS 5-5
AND WHEN I'M IN A PLAYFUL MOOD, THAT CAN MEAN ONLY ONE THING!
© 1995 PAWS, INC./Distributed by Universal Press Syndicate
CHESS BY MAIL!

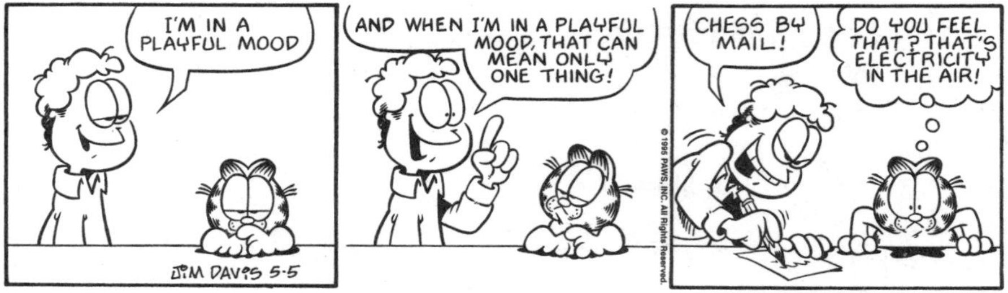
I'M IN A PLAYFUL MOOD
JIM DAVIS 5-5
AND WHEN I'M IN A PLAYFUL MOOD, THAT CAN MEAN ONLY ONE THING!
© 1995 PAWS, INC. All Rights Reserved.
CHESS BY MAIL!
DO YOU FEEL THAT? THAT'S ELECTRICITY IN THE AIR!

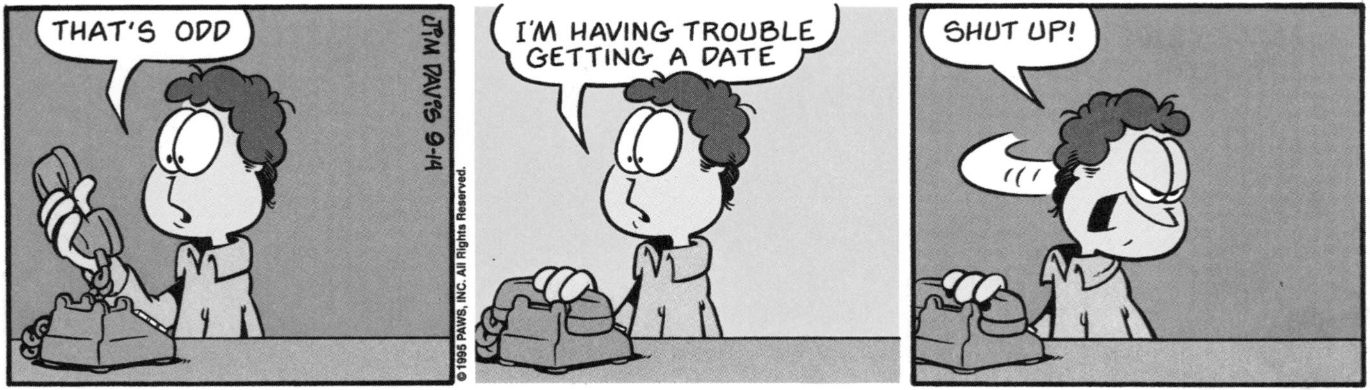
THAT'S ODD
JIM DAVIS 9-14
© 1995 PAWS, INC. All Rights Reserved.
I'M HAVING TROUBLE GETTING A DATE
SHUT UP!

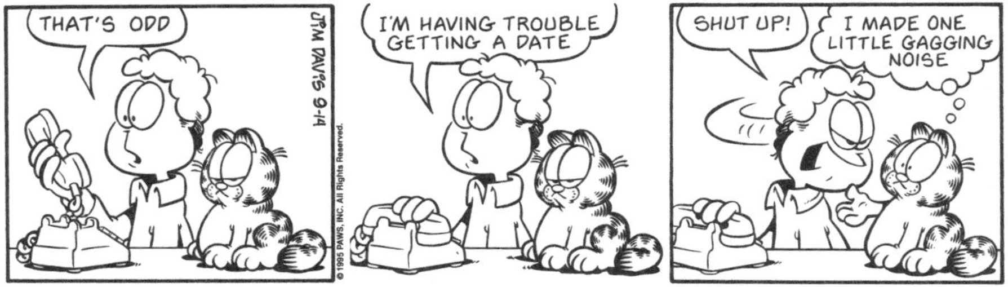
THAT'S ODD
JIM DAVIS 9-14
© 1995 PAWS, INC. All Rights Reserved.
I'M HAVING TROUBLE GETTING A DATE
SHUT UP!
I MADE ONE LITTLE GAGGING NOISE

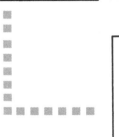

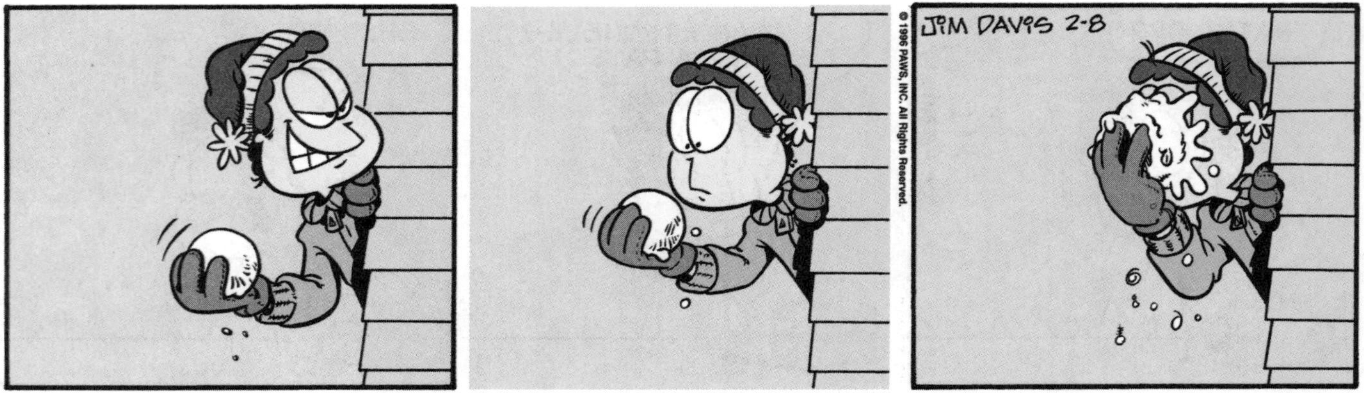
© 1996 PAWS, INC. All Rights Reserved.
JIM DAVIS 2-8

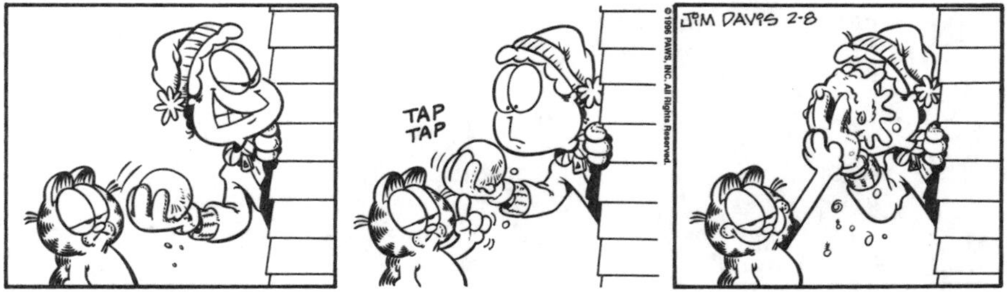
TAP
TAP
© 1996 PAWS, INC. All Rights Reserved.
JIM DAVIS 2-8

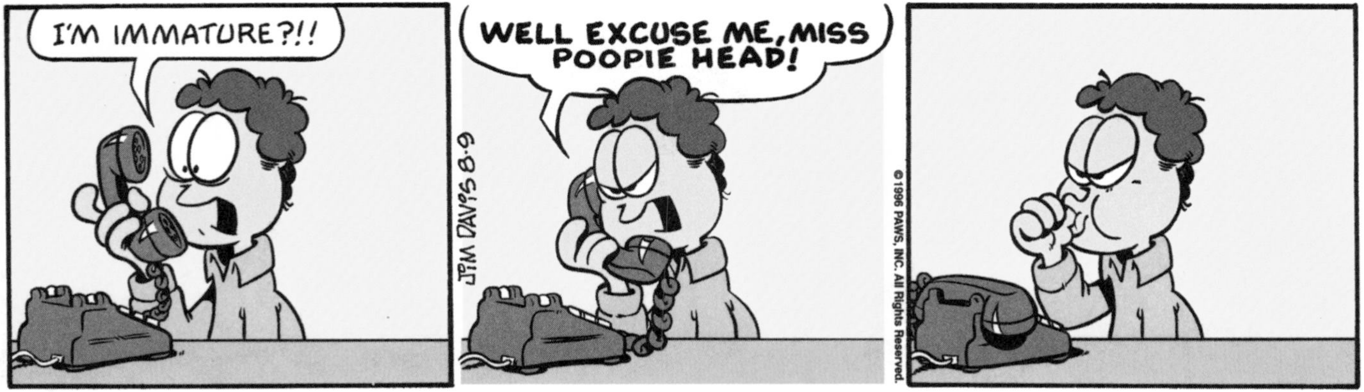
I'M IMMATURE?!!
WELL EXCUSE ME, MISS POOPIE HEAD!
JIM DAVIS 8-9
© 1996 PAWS, INC. All Rights Reserved.

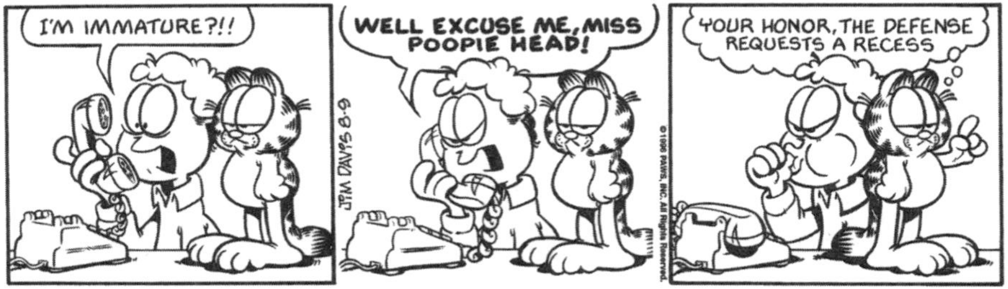
I'M IMMATURE?!!
WELL EXCUSE ME, MISS POOPIE HEAD!
YOUR HONOR, THE DEFENSE REQUESTS A RECESS
JIM DAVIS 8-9
© 1996 PAWS, INC. All Rights Reserved.

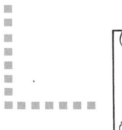

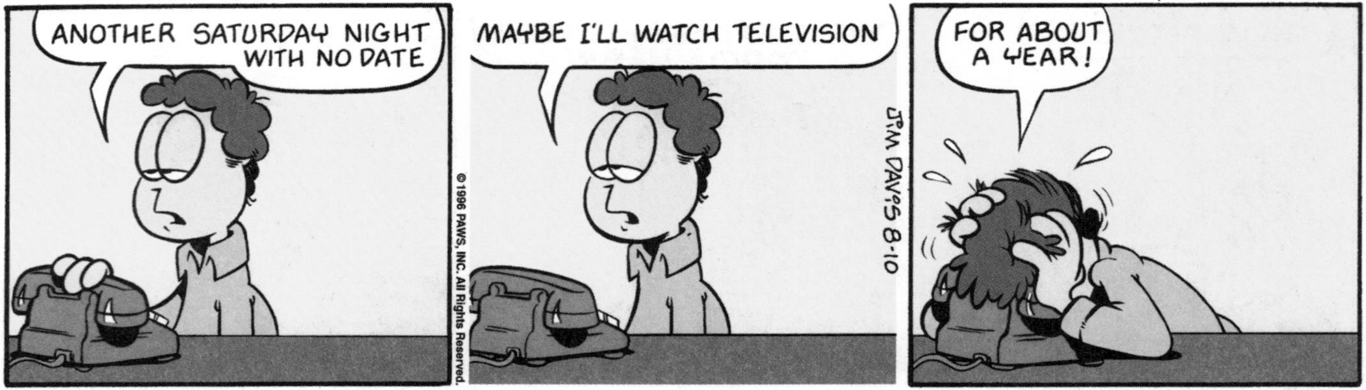
ANOTHER SATURDAY NIGHT WITH NO DATE
© 1996 PAWS, INC. All Rights Reserved.
MAYBE I'LL WATCH TELEVISION
JIM DAVIS 8-10
FOR ABOUT A YEAR!

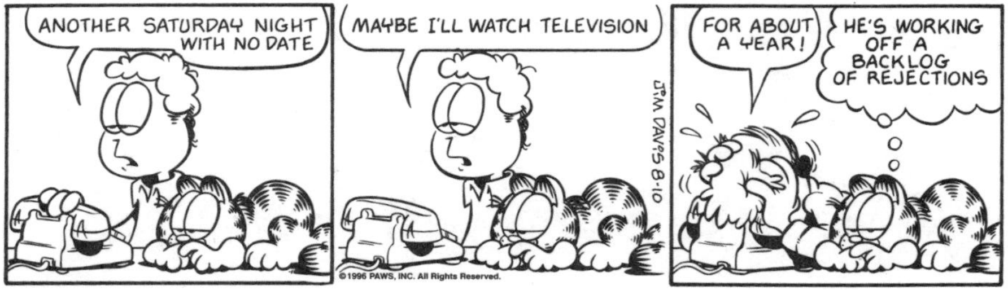
ANOTHER SATURDAY NIGHT WITH NO DATE
MAYBE I'LL WATCH TELEVISION
JIM DAVIS 8-10
© 1996 PAWS, INC. All Rights Reserved.
FOR ABOUT A YEAR!
HE'S WORKING OFF A BACKLOG OF REJECTIONS

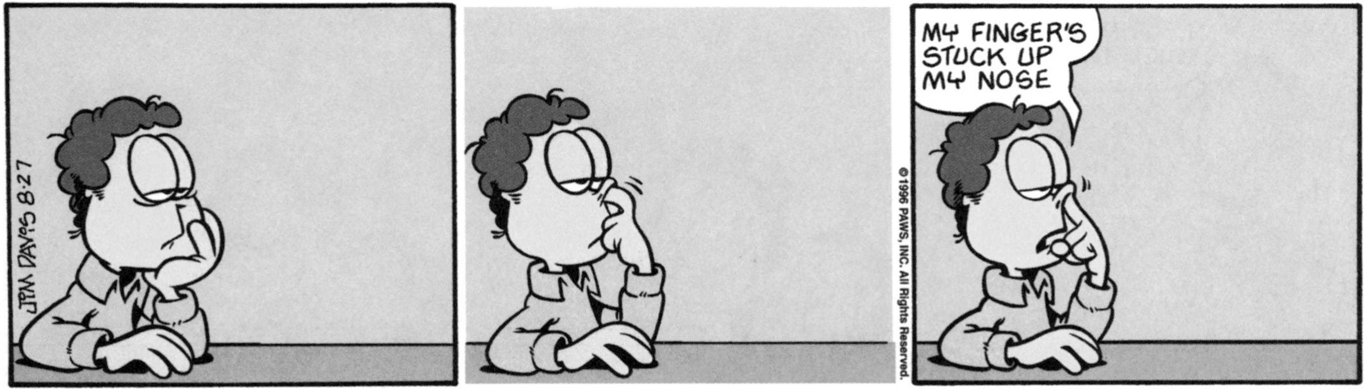
JPM DAVIS 8·27
© 1996 PAWS, INC. All Rights Reserved.
MY FINGER'S STUCK UP MY NOSE

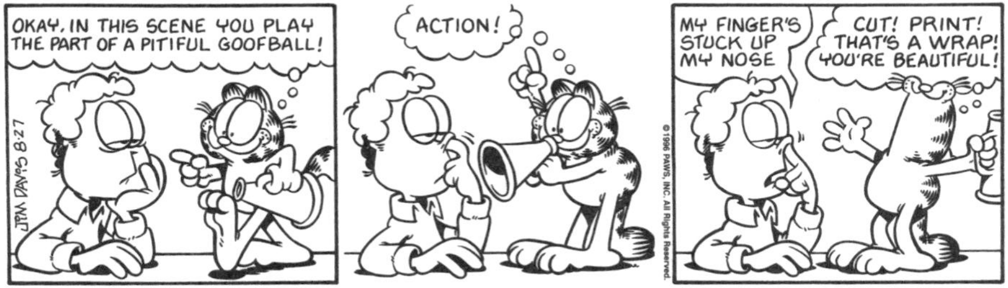
OKAY, IN THIS SCENE YOU PLAY THE PART OF A PITIFUL GOOFBALL!
JPM DAVIS 8·27
ACTION!
© 1996 PAWS, INC. All Rights Reserved.
MY FINGER'S STUCK UP MY NOSE
CUT! PRINT! THAT'S A WRAP! YOU'RE BEAUTIFUL!

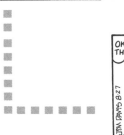

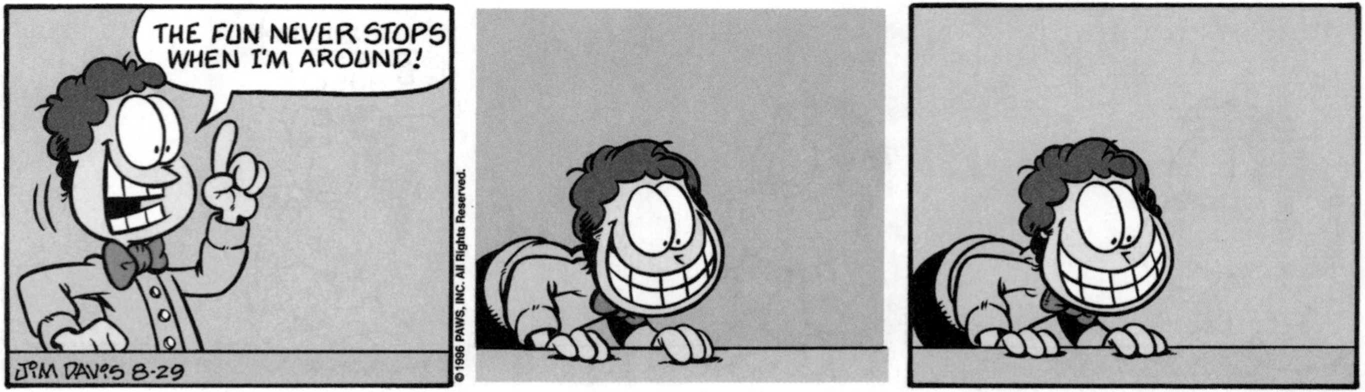
THE FUN NEVER STOPS WHEN I'M AROUND!
JIM DAVIS 8-29
©1996 PAWS, INC. All Rights Reserved.

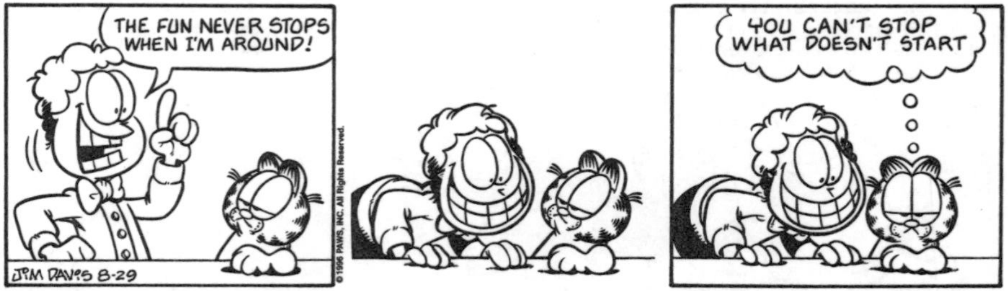
THE FUN NEVER STOPS WHEN I'M AROUND!
JIM DAVIS 8-29
©1996 PAWS, INC. All Rights Reserved.
YOU CAN'T STOP WHAT DOESN'T START

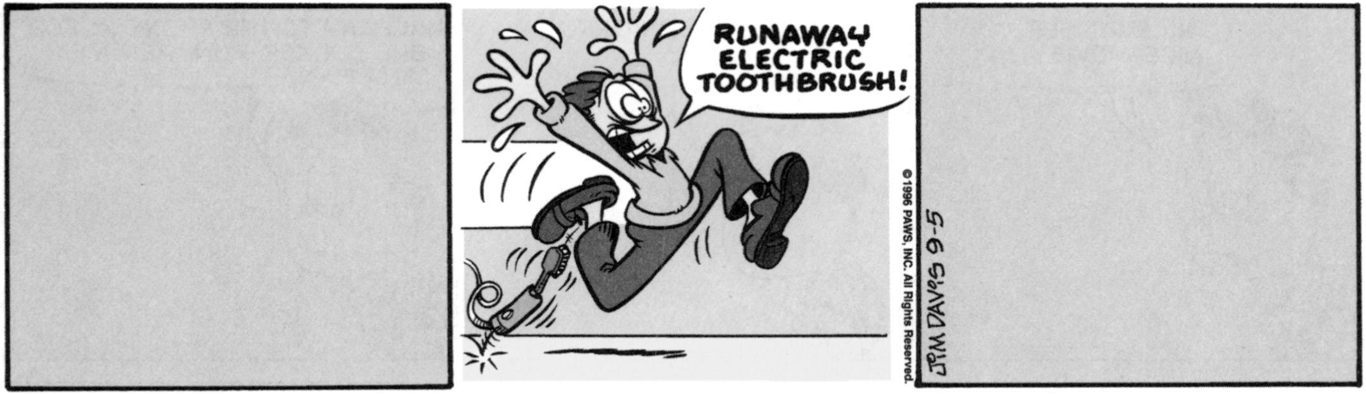
RUNAWAY ELECTRIC TOOTHBRUSH!
© 1996 PAWS, INC. All Rights Reserved.
JIM DAVIS 9-5

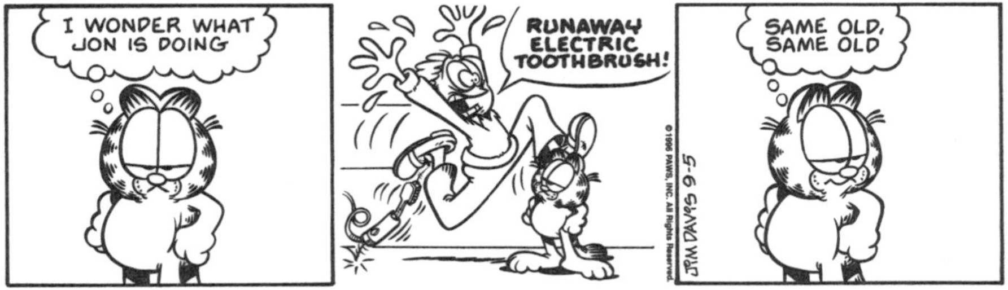
I WONDER WHAT JON IS DOING
RUNAWAY ELECTRIC TOOTHBRUSH!
© 1996 PAWS, INC. All Rights Reserved.
JIM DAVIS 9-5
SAME OLD, SAME OLD

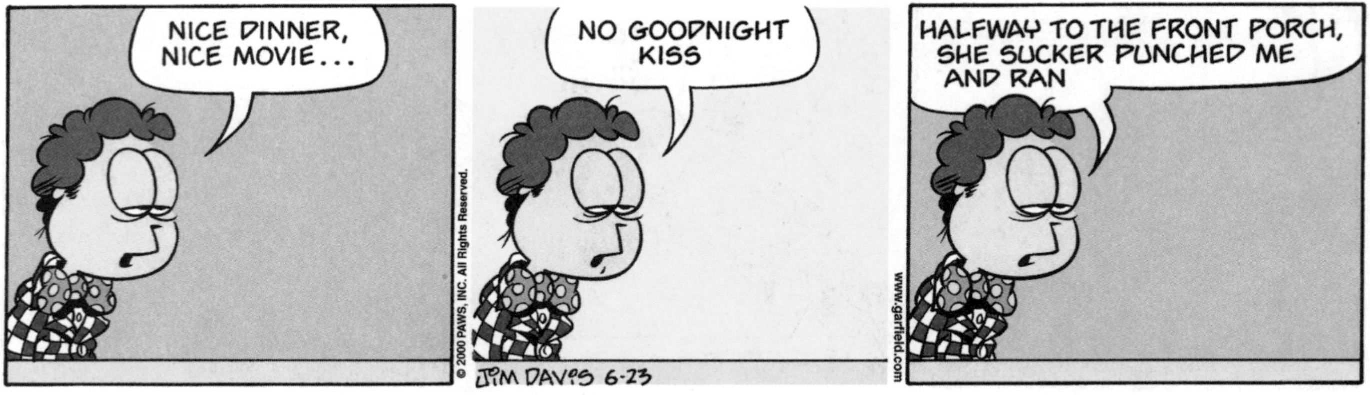
NICE DINNER, NICE MOVIE...
NO GOODNIGHT KISS
HALFWAY TO THE FRONT PORCH, SHE SUCKER PUNCHED ME AND RAN
© 2000 PAWS, INC. All Rights Reserved.
JIM DAVIS 6-23
www.garfield.com

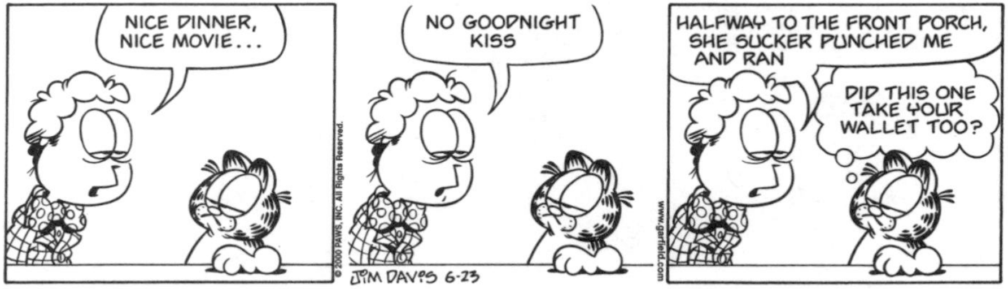
NICE DINNER, NICE MOVIE...
NO GOODNIGHT KISS
HALFWAY TO THE FRONT PORCH, SHE SUCKER PUNCHED ME AND RAN
DID THIS ONE TAKE YOUR WALLET TOO?
© 2000 PAWS, INC. All Rights Reserved.
JIM DAVIS 6-23
www.garfield.com

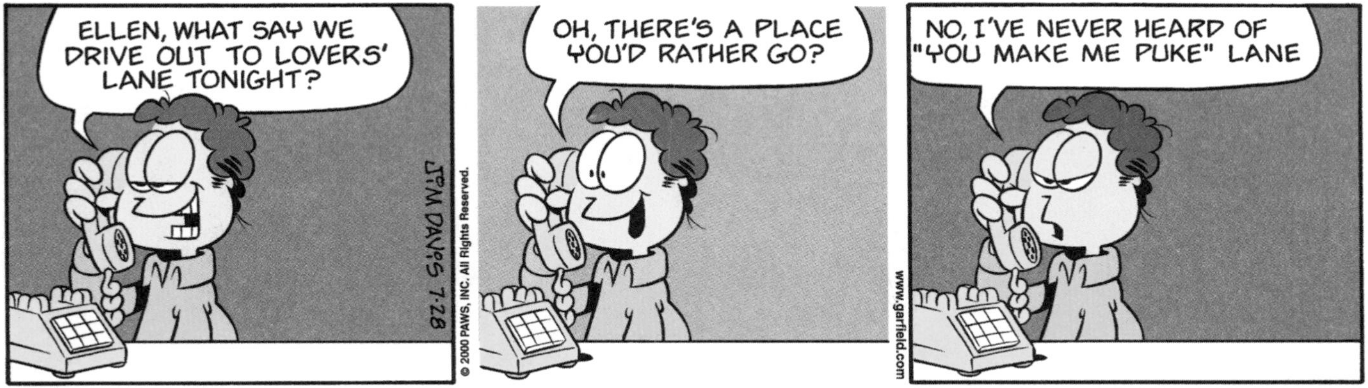
ELLEN, WHAT SAY WE DRIVE OUT TO LOVERS' LANE TONIGHT?
JIM DAVIS 7-28
© 2000 PAWS, INC. All Rights Reserved.
OH, THERE'S A PLACE YOU'D RATHER GO?
www.garfield.com
NO, I'VE NEVER HEARD OF "YOU MAKE ME PUKE" LANE

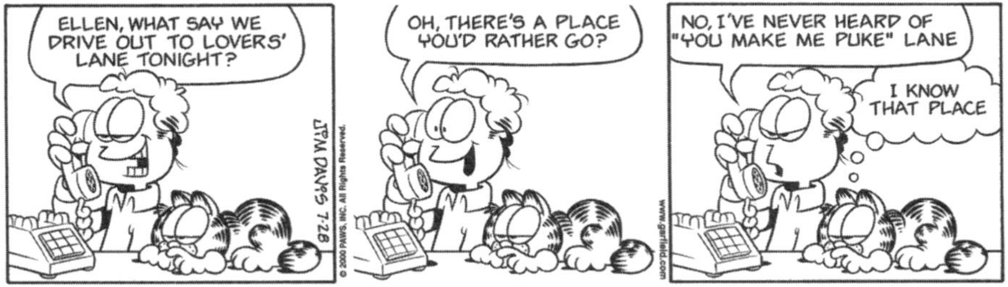
ELLEN, WHAT SAY WE DRIVE OUT TO LOVERS' LANE TONIGHT?
JIM DAVIS 7-28
© 2000 PAWS, INC. All Rights Reserved.
OH, THERE'S A PLACE YOU'D RATHER GO?
www.garfield.com
NO, I'VE NEVER HEARD OF "YOU MAKE ME PUKE" LANE
I KNOW THAT PLACE

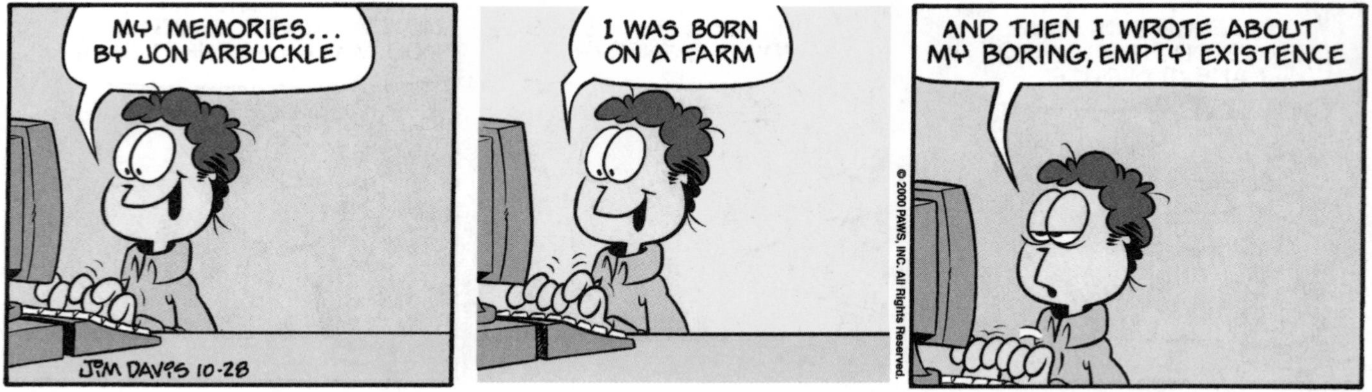
MY MEMORIES...
BY JON ARBUCKLE
JIM DAVIS 10-28
I WAS BORN
ON A FARM
© 2000 PAWS, INC. All Rights Reserved.
AND THEN I WROTE ABOUT
MY BORING, EMPTY EXISTENCE

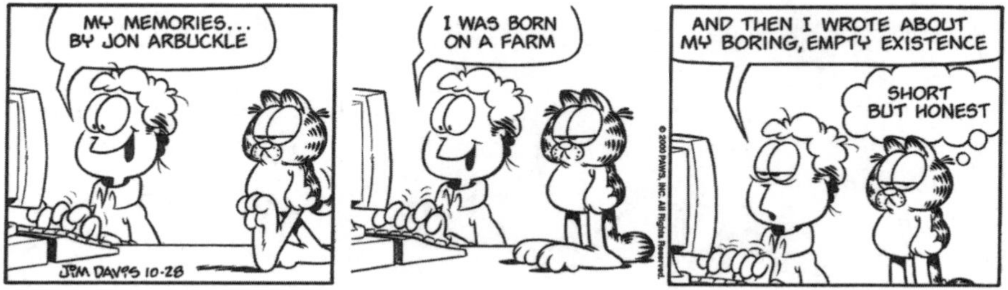
MY MEMORIES...
BY JON ARBUCKLE
JIM DAVIS 10-28
I WAS BORN
ON A FARM
AND THEN I WROTE ABOUT
MY BORING, EMPTY EXISTENCE
SHORT
BUT HONEST

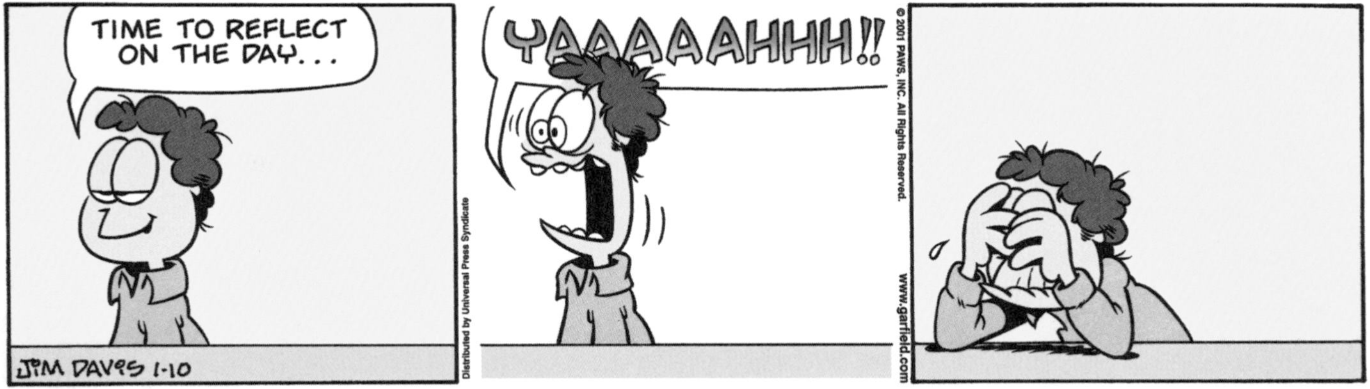
TIME TO REFLECT ON THE DAY. . .
YAAAAAHHH!!
JIM DAVIS 1-10
Distributed by Universal Press Syndicate
© 2001 PAWS, INC. All Rights Reserved.
www.garfield.com

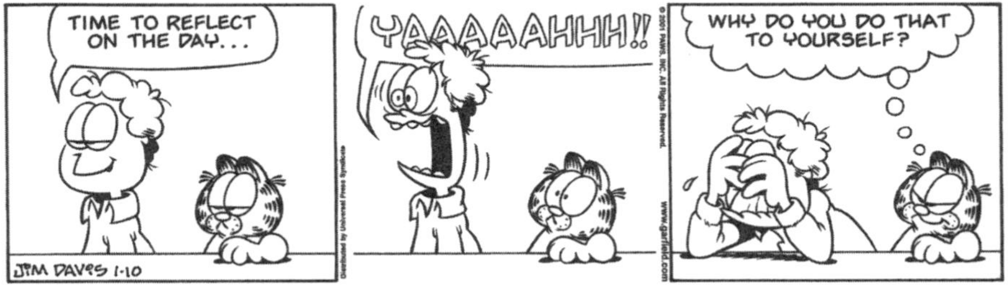
TIME TO REFLECT ON THE DAY. . .
YAAAAAHHH!!
WHY DO YOU DO THAT TO YOURSELF?
JIM DAVIS 1-10

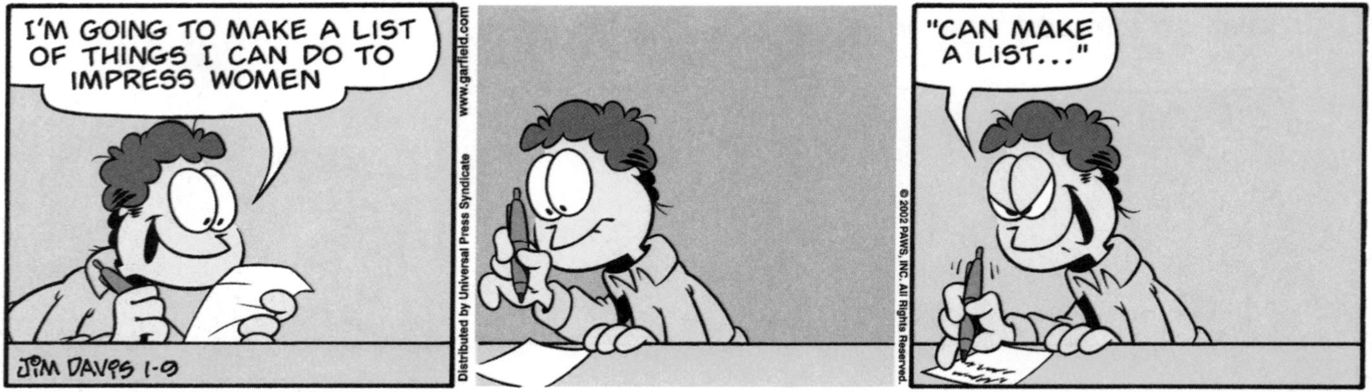
I'M GOING TO MAKE A LIST OF THINGS I CAN DO TO IMPRESS WOMEN
JIM DAVIS 1-9
Distributed by Universal Press Syndicate www.garfield.com
"CAN MAKE A LIST..."
© 2002 PAWS, INC. All Rights Reserved.

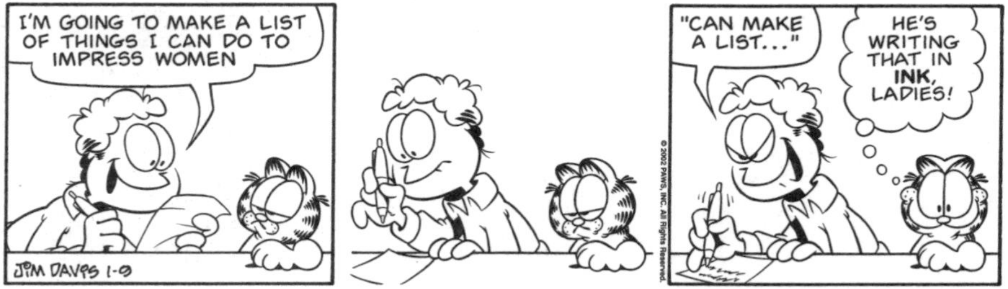
I'M GOING TO MAKE A LIST OF THINGS I CAN DO TO IMPRESS WOMEN
JIM DAVIS 1-9
"CAN MAKE A LIST..."
HE'S WRITING THAT IN **INK**, LADIES!

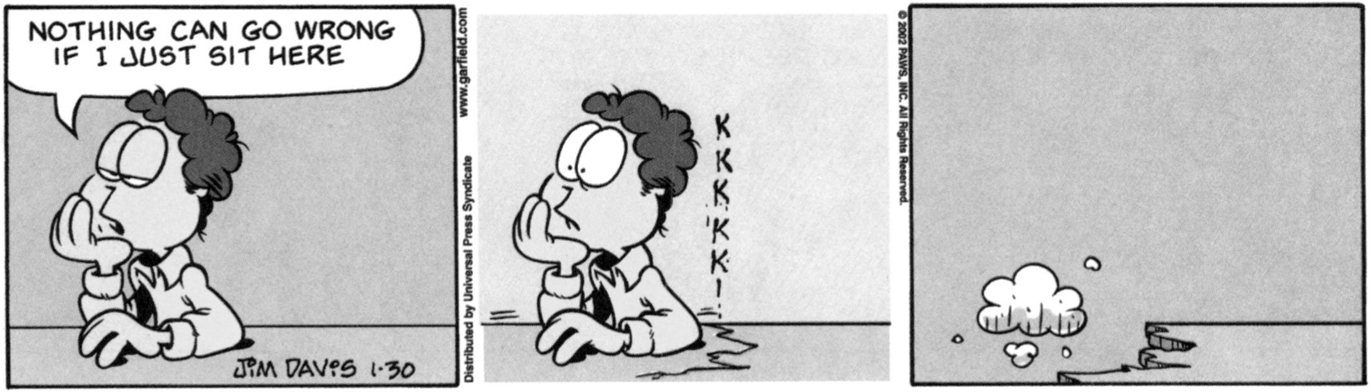
NOTHING CAN GO WRONG IF I JUST SIT HERE
JIM DAVIS 1-30
www.garfield.com
Distributed by Universal Press Syndicate
KKKKK!
© 2002 PAWS, INC. All Rights Reserved.

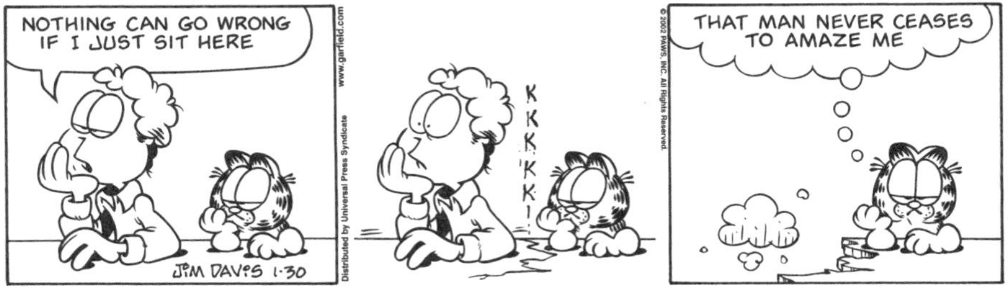
NOTHING CAN GO WRONG IF I JUST SIT HERE
JIM DAVIS 1-30
www.garfield.com
Distributed by Universal Press Syndicate
KKKKK!
© 2002 PAWS, INC. All Rights Reserved.
THAT MAN NEVER CEASES TO AMAZE ME

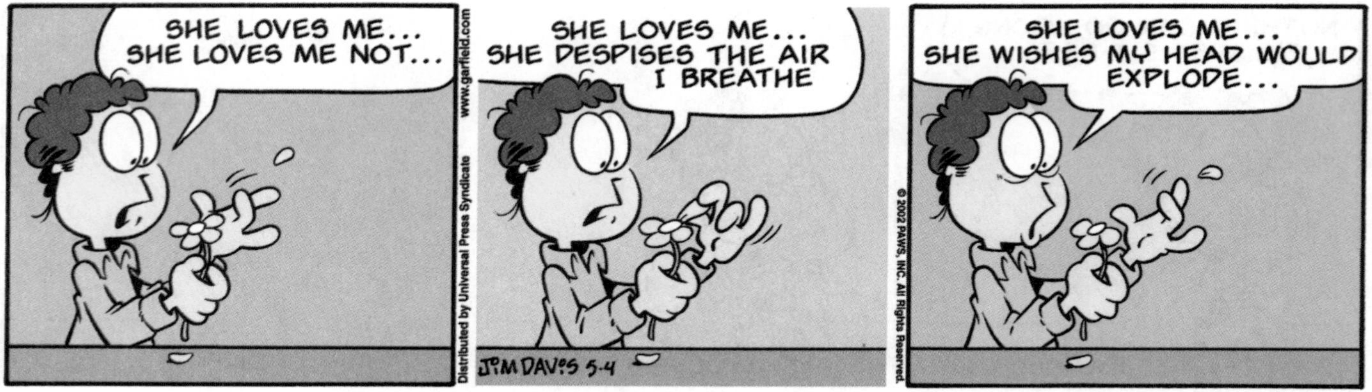
SHE LOVES ME...
SHE LOVES ME NOT...
www.garfield.com
Distributed by Universal Press Syndicate
SHE LOVES ME...
SHE DESPISES THE AIR I BREATHE
JIM DAVIS 5-4
SHE LOVES ME...
SHE WISHES MY HEAD WOULD EXPLODE...
© 2002 PAWS, INC. All Rights Reserved.

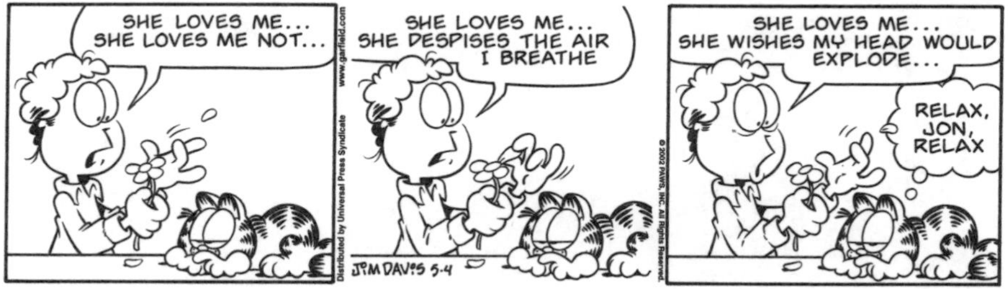
SHE LOVES ME...
SHE LOVES ME NOT...
www.garfield.com
Distributed by Universal Press Syndicate
SHE LOVES ME...
SHE DESPISES THE AIR I BREATHE
JIM DAVIS 5-4
SHE LOVES ME...
SHE WISHES MY HEAD WOULD EXPLODE...
RELAX, JON, RELAX

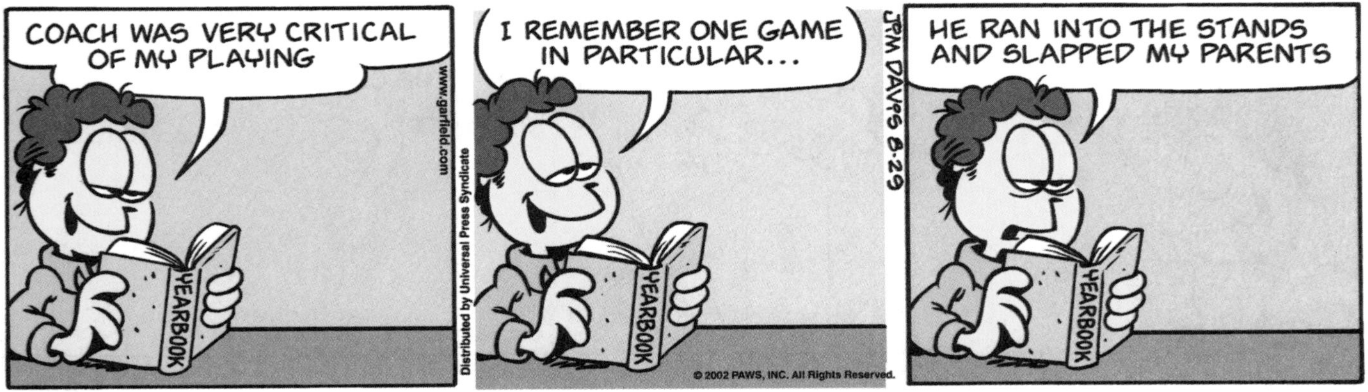
COACH WAS VERY CRITICAL OF MY PLAYING
I REMEMBER ONE GAME IN PARTICULAR...
HE RAN INTO THE STANDS AND SLAPPED MY PARENTS
YEARBOOK
JPM DAVIS 8-29
www.garfield.com
Distributed by Universal Press Syndicate
© 2002 PAWS, INC. All Rights Reserved.

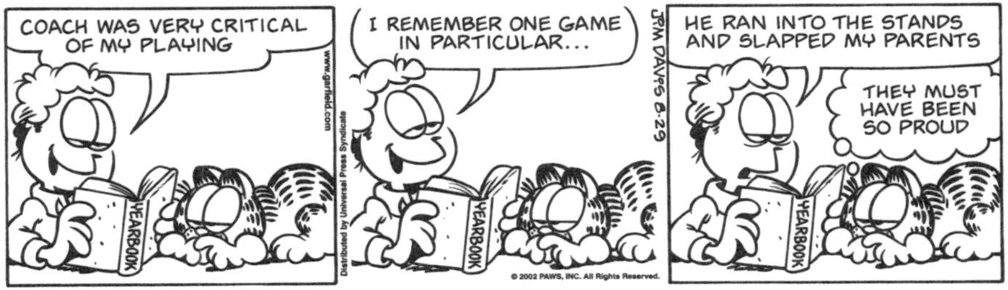
COACH WAS VERY CRITICAL OF MY PLAYING
I REMEMBER ONE GAME IN PARTICULAR...
HE RAN INTO THE STANDS AND SLAPPED MY PARENTS
THEY MUST HAVE BEEN SO PROUD
YEARBOOK
JPM DAVIS 8-29
www.garfield.com
Distributed by Universal Press Syndicate
© 2002 PAWS, INC. All Rights Reserved.

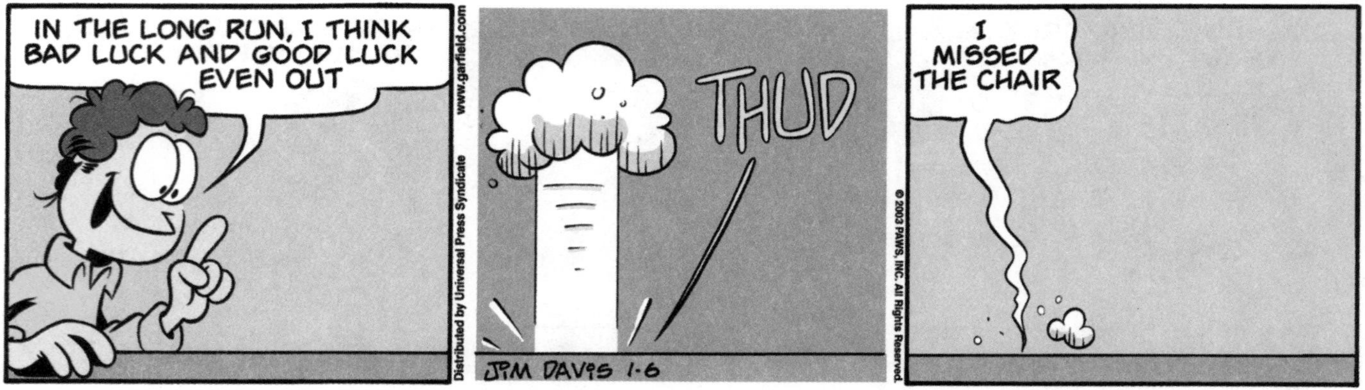
IN THE LONG RUN, I THINK BAD LUCK AND GOOD LUCK EVEN OUT
www.garfield.com
Distributed by Universal Press Syndicate
THUD
JIM DAVIS 1-6
© 2003 PAWS, INC. All Rights Reserved.
I MISSED THE CHAIR

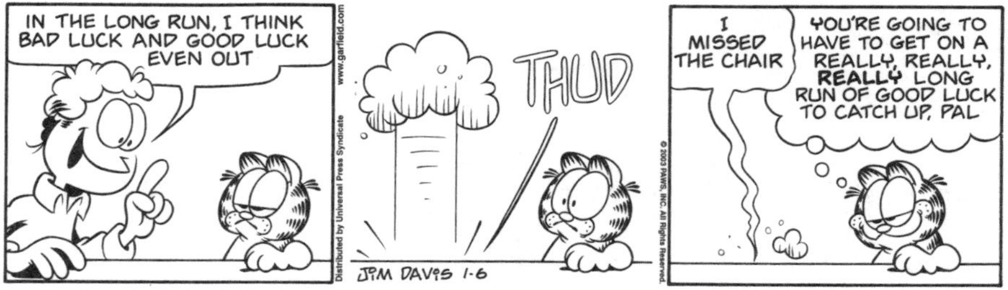
IN THE LONG RUN, I THINK BAD LUCK AND GOOD LUCK EVEN OUT
www.garfield.com
Distributed by Universal Press Syndicate
THUD
JIM DAVIS 1-6
© 2003 PAWS, INC. All Rights Reserved.
I MISSED THE CHAIR
YOU'RE GOING TO HAVE TO GET ON A REALLY, REALLY, **REALLY** LONG RUN OF GOOD LUCK TO CATCH UP, PAL

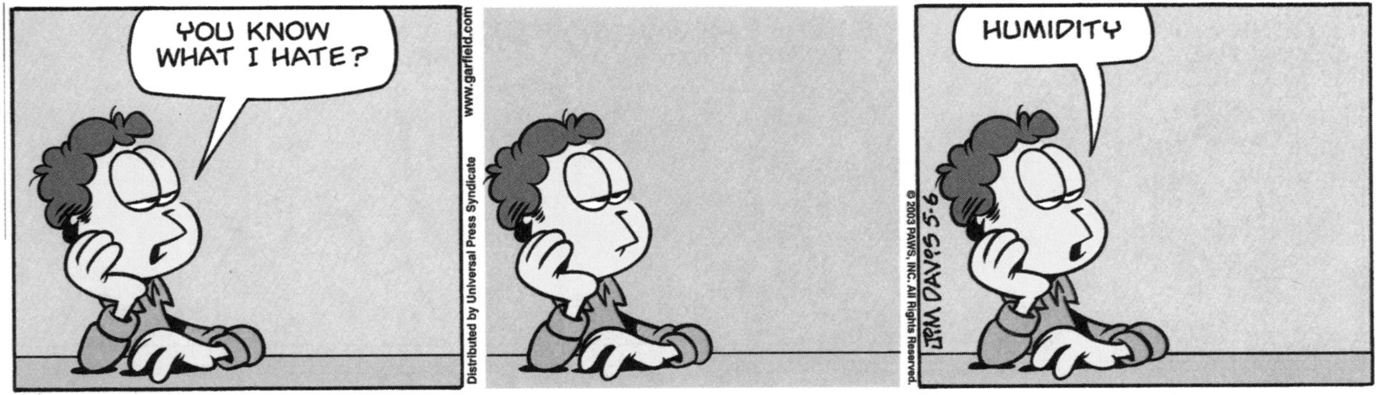
YOU KNOW WHAT I HATE?
www.garfield.com
Distributed by Universal Press Syndicate
HUMIDITY
JPM DAVIS 5-6
© 2003 PAWS, INC. All Rights Reserved.

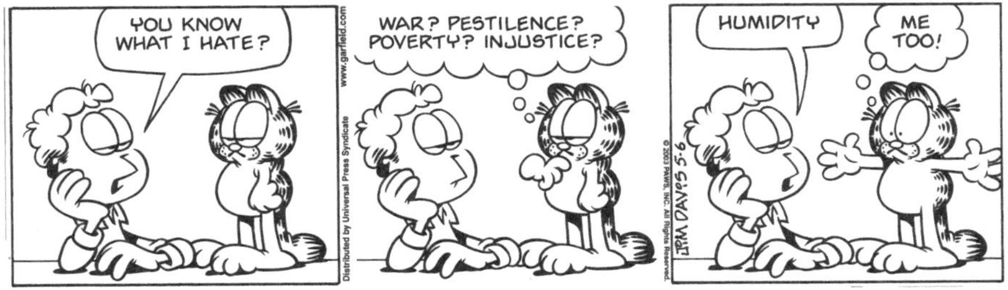
YOU KNOW WHAT I HATE?
WAR? PESTILENCE? POVERTY? INJUSTICE?
HUMIDITY
ME TOO!

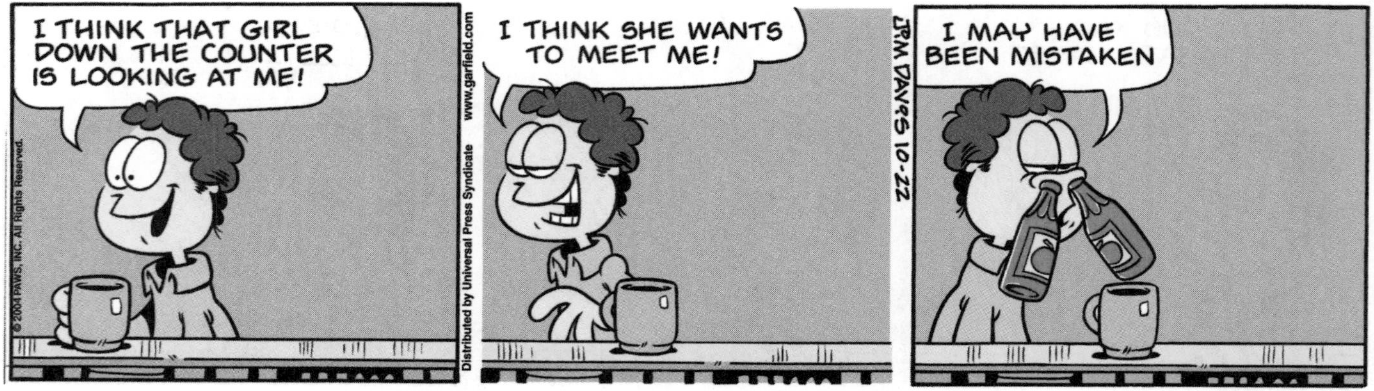
I THINK THAT GIRL DOWN THE COUNTER IS LOOKING AT ME!
© 2004 PAWS, INC. All Rights Reserved.
www.garfield.com
Distributed by Universal Press Syndicate
I THINK SHE WANTS TO MEET ME!
JIM DAVIS 10-22
I MAY HAVE BEEN MISTAKEN

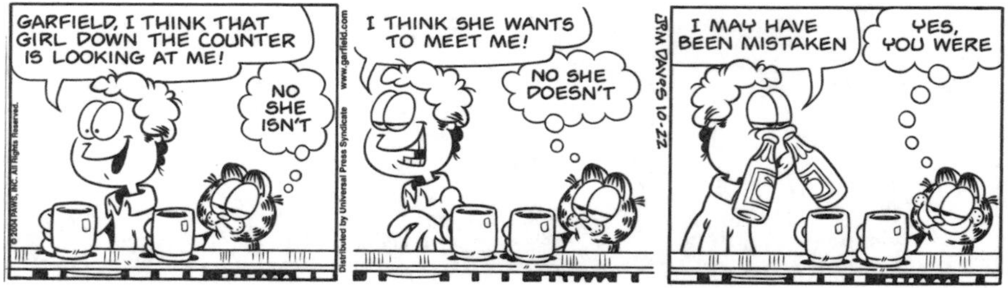
GARFIELD, I THINK THAT GIRL DOWN THE COUNTER IS LOOKING AT ME!
NO SHE ISN'T
I THINK SHE WANTS TO MEET ME!
NO SHE DOESN'T
JIM DAVIS 10-22
I MAY HAVE BEEN MISTAKEN
YES, YOU WERE

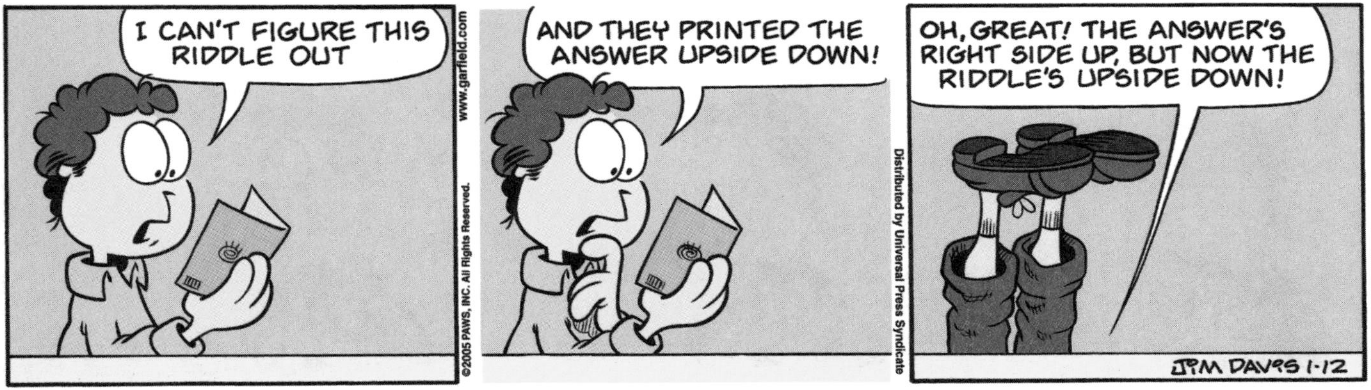
I CAN'T FIGURE THIS RIDDLE OUT
www.garfield.com
©2005 PAWS, INC. All Rights Reserved.
AND THEY PRINTED THE ANSWER UPSIDE DOWN!
Distributed by Universal Press Syndicate
OH, GREAT! THE ANSWER'S RIGHT SIDE UP, BUT NOW THE RIDDLE'S UPSIDE DOWN!
JIM DAVIS 1-12

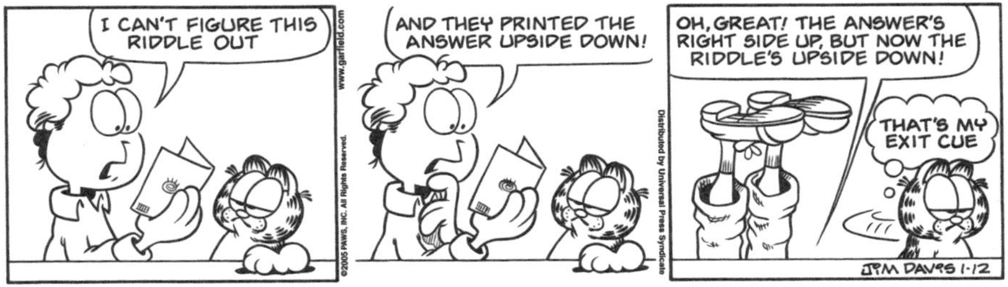
I CAN'T FIGURE THIS RIDDLE OUT
www.garfield.com
©2005 PAWS, INC. All Rights Reserved.
AND THEY PRINTED THE ANSWER UPSIDE DOWN!
Distributed by Universal Press Syndicate
OH, GREAT! THE ANSWER'S RIGHT SIDE UP, BUT NOW THE RIDDLE'S UPSIDE DOWN!
THAT'S MY EXIT CUE
JIM DAVIS 1-12

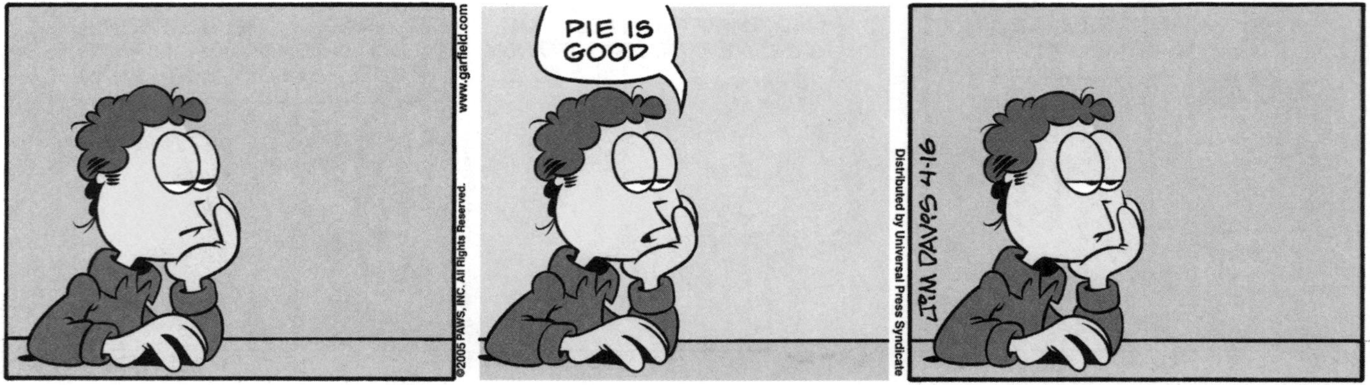
www.garfield.com
©2005 PAWS, INC. All Rights Reserved.
PIE IS GOOD
Distributed by Universal Press Syndicate
JIM DAVIS 4-16

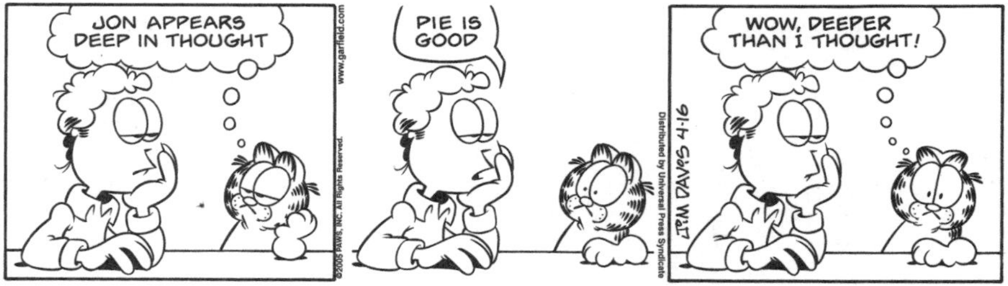
JON APPEARS DEEP IN THOUGHT
www.garfield.com
©2005 PAWS, INC. All Rights Reserved.
PIE IS GOOD
Distributed by Universal Press Syndicate
JIM DAVIS 4-16
WOW, DEEPER THAN I THOUGHT!

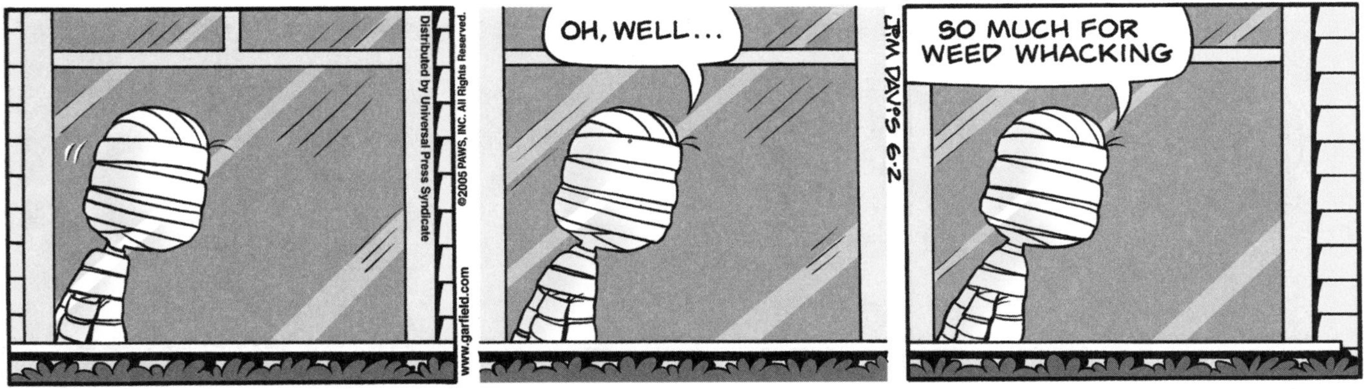
©2005 PAWS, INC. All Rights Reserved.
Distributed by Universal Press Syndicate
www.garfield.com
OH, WELL...
JIM DAVIS 6-2
SO MUCH FOR WEED WHACKING

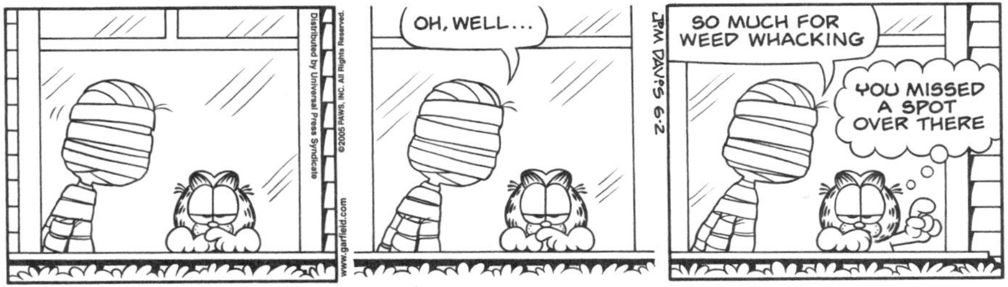
©2005 PAWS, INC. All Rights Reserved.
Distributed by Universal Press Syndicate
www.garfield.com
OH, WELL...
JIM DAVIS 6-2
SO MUCH FOR WEED WHACKING
YOU MISSED A SPOT OVER THERE

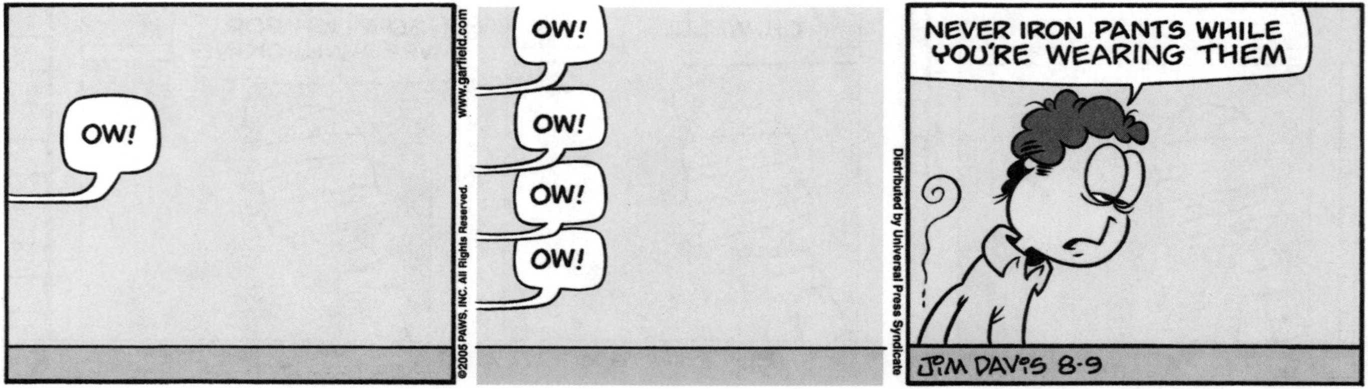
OW!
OW!
OW!
OW!
OW!
NEVER IRON PANTS WHILE YOU'RE WEARING THEM
©2005 PAWS, INC. All Rights Reserved. www.garfield.com
Distributed by Universal Press Syndicate
JIM DAVIS 8-9

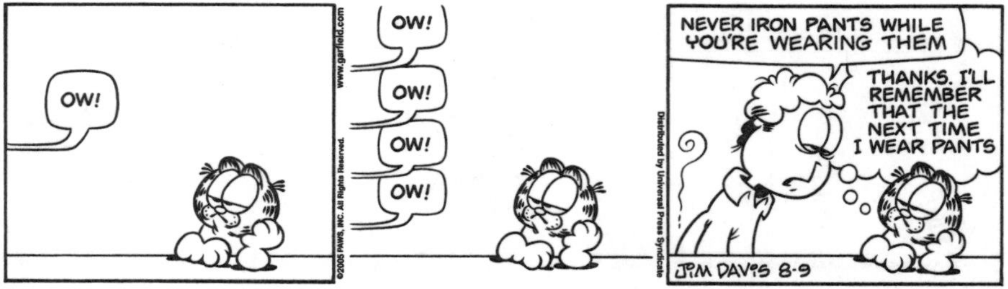
OW!
OW!
OW!
OW!
OW!
NEVER IRON PANTS WHILE YOU'RE WEARING THEM
THANKS. I'LL REMEMBER THAT THE NEXT TIME I WEAR PANTS
©2005 PAWS, INC. All Rights Reserved. www.garfield.com
Distributed by Universal Press Syndicate
JIM DAVIS 8-9

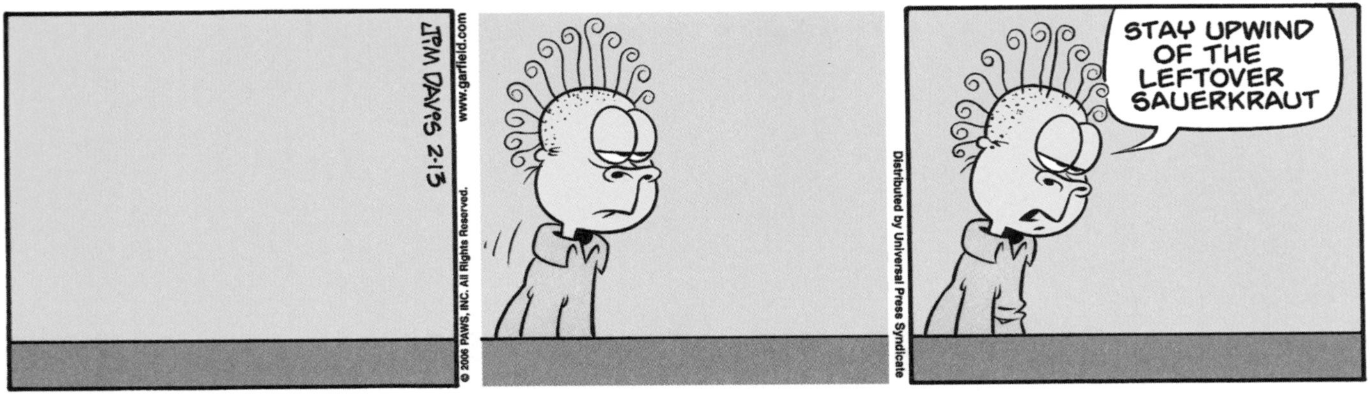
www.garfield.com
© 2006 PAWS, INC. All Rights Reserved.
Distributed by Universal Press Syndicate
STAY UPWIND OF THE LEFTOVER SAUERKRAUT

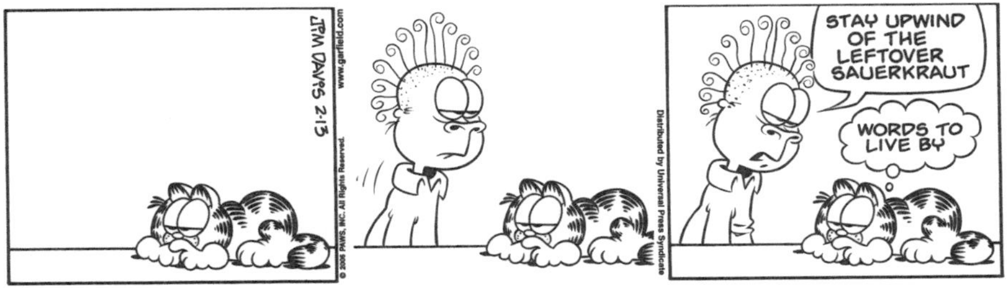
www.garfield.com
© 2006 PAWS, INC. All Rights Reserved.
Distributed by Universal Press Syndicate
STAY UPWIND OF THE LEFTOVER SAUERKRAUT
WORDS TO LIVE BY

GARFIELD-MINUS-GARFIELD PRODUCTS YOU WON'T BE SEEING

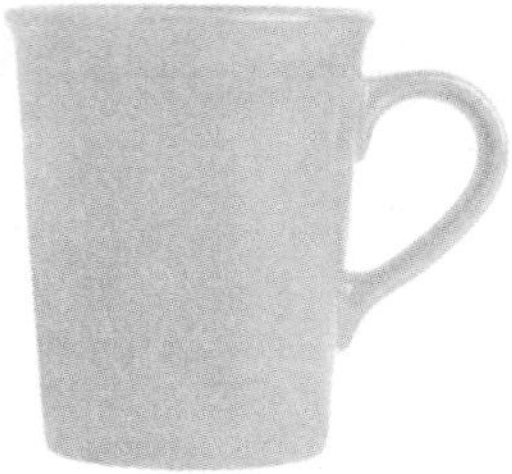

MUG

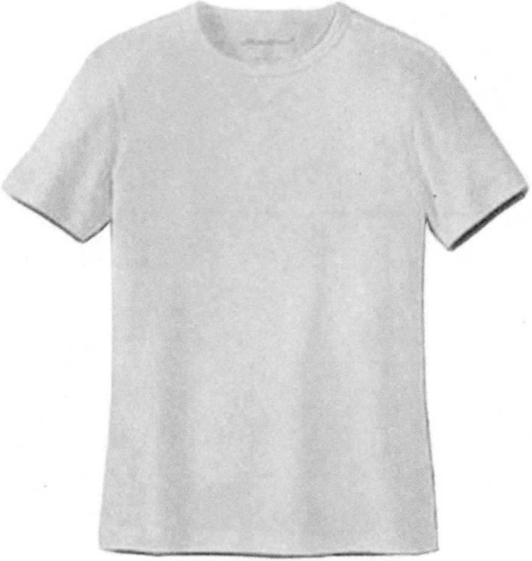

T-SHIRT

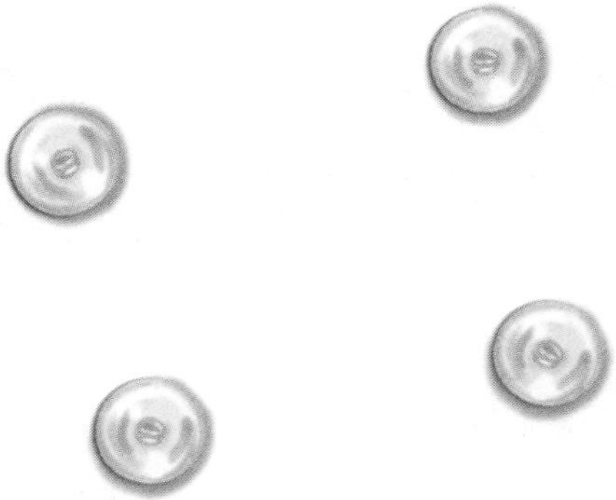

SUCTION-CUP DOLL

THE NEXT SENSATION?!

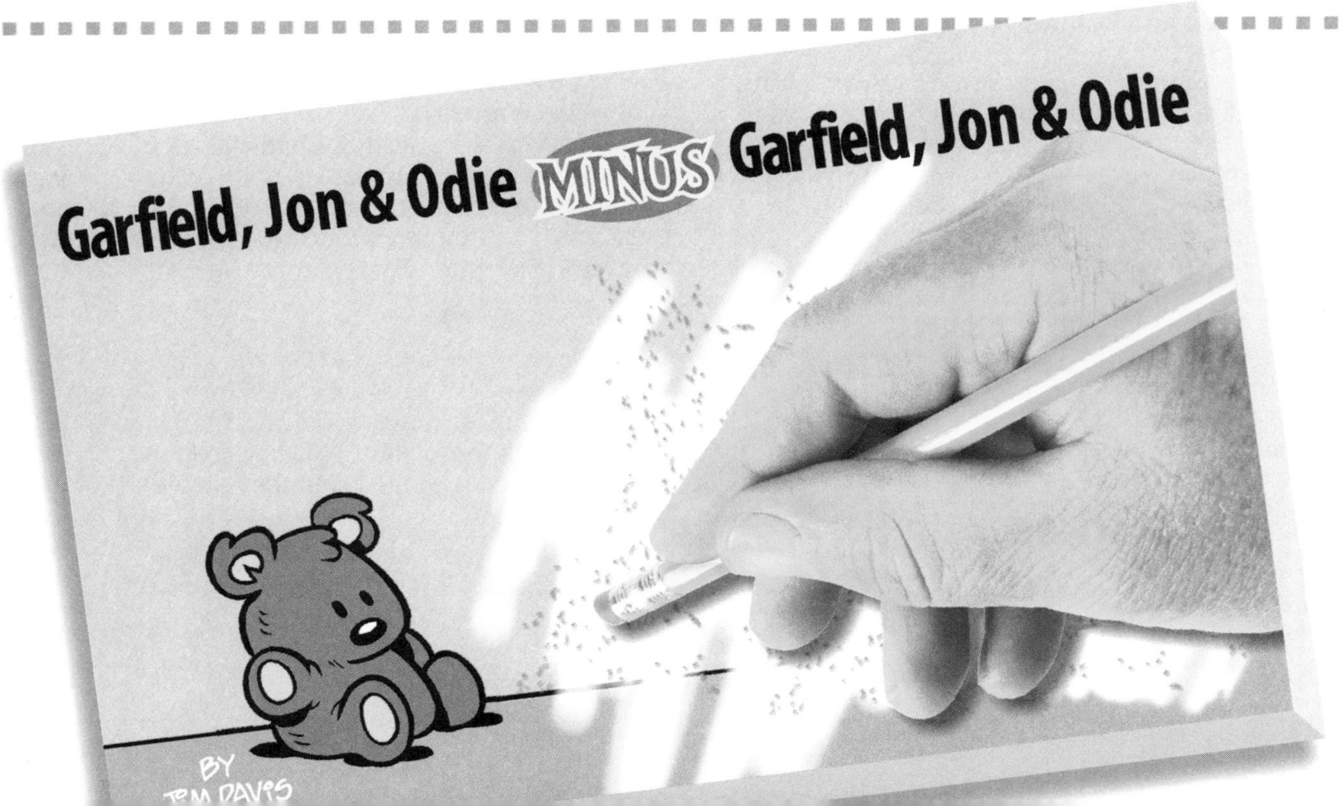
Garfield, Jon & Odie MINUS Garfield, Jon & Odie
BY
TOM DAVIS

About the Authors

Dan Walsh is a thirty-three-year-old musician, artist, nerd, and businessman from Dublin, Ireland. He attended Sandymount High School and then went on to study art. He regularly sold his paintings at St. Stephen's Green Park, where he could be found drinking coffee, playing guitar, and writing.

His foray into writing comics started when he was ten years old. He would draw his own comic books with several endings so that the reader could decide how each story concluded. A long career as a musician and an artist and an eventual move into business as an Information Technology project manager spurred Dan into revisting his childhood passion for comics, and garfieldminusgarfield.net was born.

He now lives in Dublin city center with his fiancée, Yvonne, and two dwarf hamsters, Punchy and Fat-head.

Jim Davis was born on July 28, 1945 in Marion, Indiana. He attended Ball State University in Muncie, Indiana, where he distinguished himself by earning one of the lowest cumulative grade point averages in the history of the university. (Incidentally, a fellow classmate named David Letterman earned the other.) Davis is the author of thirty-three *New York Times* bestsellers.

Garfield was born on June 19, 1978, and was syndicated in 41 U.S. newspapers. Today *Garfield* is the world's most widely syndicated comic strip, appearing in more than 2,400 newspapers with some 200 million readers in 111 countries around the globe.